The Misadventures of Hansje

The Boy Who Kept His Guardian Angel Busy

Jack Popjes

The Misadventures of Hansje

Chapter illustrations, Cover Art and Design by Micayla Jones and Kierra Jones

Formatting by Wild Seas Formatting

ISBN-13: 978-1545391358

ISBN-10: 1545391351

The WordMan

Table of Contents

1 The Very Beginning of Hansje

This is the first story in the book about a boy named Hansje. [HAHN-sjuh] But this first story is not about him. It's about some other people, some very important people. If it weren't for these two people there wouldn't even be a Hansje, so that's why I'm telling their story first. Here it is:

Long, long ago in a far-away country called Holland, there lived a lovely girl named Aaltje. [ALL-tjuh] She was about nineteen years old, and she was a nice girl, quite short, and very cute. But she was also very lonely because she lived and worked far away

1

from her dad and mom in a different part of Holland where people didn't even speak Aaltje's language.

Aaltje's family lived in a part of Holland called Friesland. [FREES-land] The people in Friesland spoke Frisian which is not like the language they speak in the rest of Holland. Friesland had lots of big farms with cows and fields. But Aaltje's family didn't own a farm. No, they lived in a small house in town, and their dad didn't have a good job, so they were very poor. When Aaltje was about twelve years old, her Mom said,

"Aaltje, you have been going to school for six years. You know how to read and write, and you can do arithmetic. Now we need you to quit school and go to work and earn some money to help buy food for yourself and the rest of the family."

Aaltje wasn't surprised because all her school friends from poor families were also quitting school after grade six and going to work.

So Aaltje started working as a housecleaner and dishwasher in a rich person's house. After a few more years, her Mom talked to her again. "Aaltje," she said, "you have another baby sister and a little brother, and we need your room. So, we need you to go and work in the same doctor's house where your older sister Anna is working."

The next week Aaltje rode a train for two hours and to the town where she would live with her older sister in the doctor's house. Anna cooked the meals, and Aaltje helped her, washed dishes and cleaned the house. Every week they got some money from the doctor and his wife, and they sent it to their dad and mom back in Friesland. They lived in the doctor's house and ate all their meals there, so they didn't have to spend any money for that.

The doctor and his wife and everyone else in town only spoke Dutch, which is the language they speak everywhere in Holland. Aaltje had learned to speak and read Dutch in school. But, of course, she spoke Frisian with her sister, which made her feel a little more at home.

One day, on her weekly afternoon off, Aaltje went riding her bike with some other girls. When they saw some boys playing with a ball in a field, they stopped to watch.

Suddenly one of the boys called to Aaltje and her friends, "Hey girls! Do you want to come and play catch with us for a while?"

"Okay!" Aaltje said, and she and her friends played catch for quite a while with those boys talking and laughing with each other.

Aaltje noticed right away that some of the boys spoke Frisian, so she spoke Frisian too. Then one tall, very handsome boy talked Frisian to her while he kept on tossing the ball to her and no one else. She was starting to like him, and when they stopped playing catch to rest for a while, she asked what his name was.

"Hans," he said and shook hands with Aaltje the way people always do in Holland.

After that, every week on her day off, Aaltje met Hans to play ball or go for a fun bike ride together, talking Frisian. "My work is buying fish from fishermen." Hans told her, "Then my dad and brothers clean the fish to sell to people. Our whole family moved from Friesland to live in Hilversum, the neighbour city not too far away from where you live."

One day, they rode up to a café with an outside area filled with small tables and chairs. So, Hans said,

"Hey, Aaltje, do you want to stop here and get something to drink?"

"Yes," Aaltje said, "I would love a glass of lemonade."

They parked their bikes in the bike rack and sat at a little table and asked the waiter for a glass of lemonade for Aaltje and a glass of beer for Hans. After they had taken a few sips, Hans said, "Excuse me a minute, I need to use the washroom." He got up and went into the café to find the washroom.

As soon as he was gone, Aaltje did a very strange thing. She set down her glass of lemonade and picked up the tall glass of beer that Hans had ordered. She sniffed it and made an ugly face, then she stretched out her hand and poured the whole glass of beer onto the gravel where they were sitting. Then she put the empty glass back on the table and sat there looking innocent.

Soon Hans came back, sat down and reached for his glass. "Hey," he said, looking at Aaltje in surprise, "what happened to my beer?"

"It's down there," Aaltje said, pointing at the ground where the gravel was all wet and foamy.

Hans didn't know what to say. Finally, he asked her, "Why did you pour out my beer?"

"Hans," she said, "I'm starting to like you, like you

a lot. But I don't want to start being good friends with a young man who drinks beer. My older brother drank too much beer and got drunk. He acted all crazy and then he fell and threw up. It was awful. I don't ever want that to happen to someone I am good friends with. So, if you are a beer drinker, I think we should stop seeing each other."

Hans sat there listening very quietly and thinking to himself, "Wow, this girl really wants to live right. I like her ideas. And I like to hear her saying that she likes me and that if we keep on seeing each other, she may become especially good friends with me. Even though I go to church every Sunday, I haven't met any girl that has such good ideas about living right."

When Aaltje stopped talking, she wondered if Hans would get angry at her and argue, or just get on his bike and ride off, never to see her again?

Then Hans started to talk. "Well, I guess I have to explain something to you. It's like this. I, uh, also like you a lot and I was hoping you would like me, too. And I was worried that you didn't think I was a real man, someone you could be proud to be with. You know the saying around here, *You're not a real man unless you can drink beer.*"

Then he looked down in embarrassment and said, "But actually, I tasted beer once and didn't like it. I just wanted to impress you."

Aaltje liked him even more when he said that, and she laughed in relief that he wasn't angry at her. Hans laughed too and waved at the waiter to come over so he could order a lemonade as well.

After that, they met many more times, and they never went out with anyone else except each other. Hans took her home to meet his dad and his mom and his two sisters, and his six brothers and to talk Frisian with them. His family wasn't poor. No, they had a good business, buying, cleaning, and selling all kinds of fish. All the older brothers were working in the business, especially Hans since he was the oldest.

The family in which Hans grew up all went to church every Sunday, and they read the Bible at meals and prayed. This was new to Aaltje whose family didn't do those things. Well, maybe except at Christmas, then they would sometimes go to church. When she saw that Hans' family read the Bible and heard about them going to church, she thought, *I've always heard that church going people are good people. That means Hans is probably a good person. Now I really like him a lot.*

One time when Aaltje had a few day's vacation, she and Hans rode the train to Akkrum, [AHK-rum] the town where Aaltje's parents and her two brothers and younger sisters lived. The older sisters were, of course, all far away working in rich people's houses. "He seems like a nice Frisian boy," they said, "If you want to marry him, go ahead."

So not long after that, Hans and Aaltje decided to become engaged to be married. They bought gold wedding rings and wore them on the ring finger of their right hand, to show that they were engaged. All during the time that they were engaged, Aaltje worked as a housemaid and Hans worked very hard in his Dad's fish business.

Finally, after three years of being engaged and saving money, they got married. During the marriage ceremony, they moved their gold rings from the right hand to the ring finger of their left hand to show they were now married.

They lived in a small house in the city where Hans' family lived. He started his own fish cleaning and selling business and sold fish every day from a stand near a busy street. A year later a baby boy was born to Hans and Aaltje. They named him Hans, after his Dad, but because he was still very small, they called him Hansje which means 'little Hans.'

And now you know why these two people were so important to this book about Hansje.

2 Hansje and the Men Stealers

When Hansje was still little and not even going to kindergarten yet, a horrible thing happened in his country. Some very bad soldiers came from another country right next to Holland. They had big guns and big boots and big voices. There were so many of them that they chased away all the good soldiers and policemen from the city where Hansje lived.

These bad soldiers came past people's houses with big trucks and came in to steal their radios, their cars and trucks, and even their bicycles. They stole a lot of other things too, like bread from the bakeries and food from the grocery stores. They even stole machines and tools from factories and workshops. When it got cold, they stole the firewood and coal that people needed to keep warm.

That was awful. But then it got even worse.

The soldiers wanted strong men to work for them in the factories and fields far away, back in their own country, since all their strong men had become soldiers. So, they started stealing lots of daddies, uncles, big brothers, and even grandpas if they weren't too old. They locked them into train boxcars and drove those trains all the way back to their country.

There they made all those daddies, uncles, and grandpas get out and work with shovels and hoes on farms, and with machines in factories. They only got a little bit to eat. And they didn't get paid. No, they were slaves. If they didn't work hard, the soldiers beat them with sticks. And if they tried to run away the soldiers would shoot them with their guns.

One morning, when Hansje was about five years old, he came running into the house and shouted,

"Mama, Mama, can I have a big piece of bread?"

"Why? Are you hungry already?" she asked, "We

just had breakfast."

"No, it is to give to the men in the boxcars," he explained. Then he told her there was a train full of boxcars waiting in the train yard to be hooked up to an engine.

"All the boxcars have hands sticking out of the cracks in the boards, and the men are yelling inside that they are hungry, and all my friends are bringing bread to give them. Lots of the boxcars have men that say they are Jews."

Right away Mama felt sorry for those men, but she worried a bit about her little Hansje going there.

"I don't think you should go there," she said. "You're too small; I don't want you that close to the trains."

"But it's the bigger boys that are inside the fence." Hansje explained, "They're the ones running up to the boxcars to give those men the bread. I just hand it to them through the fence."

Mama knew there would be lots of bad, enemy soldiers around with big guns, but she also knew they didn't care about little kids; they only shot their guns at big people. Well, usually. So, she gave Hansje a small piece of bread, not too much because they didn't have much to eat themselves. Hansje ran off to bring bread to the hungry men in those boxcars. He didn't care if there were bad soldiers with big guns around; he had seen them all his life.

While Hansje was gone, Papa and Mama wondered what would happen if those bad soldiers came to the streets in their city to steal people.

At night, nobody was supposed to be outside on the streets except soldiers. But Hansje's uncles who lived a few blocks from Hansje's house, sneaked away out of their city one night and hid in a huge swampy place far from town. The ground was so soft and muddy that no big soldiers' trucks could drive there and there were so many lakes and islands in that place; the bad soldiers would have a hard time finding anyone there because the men hiding there had rowboats to get away and hide again.

But Papa couldn't go with the brothers because he was married and had to look after Mama, Hansje and little Jannie. So, Papa got a saw and went into the back room of their house. He dragged a heavy dish cabinet away from the wall, rolled away the carpet, and cut a square hole in the boards of the floor. Underneath the floor was a crawl space that he could creep into, to hide from the enemy soldiers if they ever came down their street to steal men.

He could crawl under the house right over to their next-door neighbour's house that was attached to theirs. If the bad soldiers came to their house and found the place where he had sawed the floor, and they started to open it, he could quickly crawl to their neighbour's house and climb out the hole they had cut in their back room. Then he could try to sneak away through their neighbour's back yard. And the neighbour could do the same thing if they came to his house. It was a good plan.

Of course, they didn't leave that hole wide open for everyone to see. Papa made a nice lid that fit right into the hole, and you could hardly see the edges. Then he put the carpet back over it, and the dish cabinet back in its place.

One day it happened. A soldier truck stopped at one end of the street, and another one stopped at the other end. Big bad soldiers got out of the trucks carrying guns and started going into houses looking for men to steal. Hansje saw them and ran home as quickly as he could.

"Papa, Mama," he shouted, "the bad soldiers are stealing men on our street!"

They all ran to the back room, and dragged the heavy dish cabinet away from the wall; then they rolled up the carpet underneath. Quickly Papa lifted the lid and crawled down under the floor. Mama put the lid back down and rolled the carpet over the lid. Then she and Hansje pushed and shoved until that big, heavy, dish cabinet was back in its place. Hansje rubbed out the tracks where the feet of the dish cabinet had dragged over the carpet so that no one would guess it had ever been moved.

Hansje already knew what to do next, because Papa and Mama had told him what to do if ever Papa had to go down underneath the floor. He set the table for three people: Mama, his little sister Jannie, and himself.

In the meantime, Mama went upstairs to the clothes closet and took down all of Papa's pants and shirts and put them in a box. She also took all his shorts, socks, and shoes, and his pillow from the bed, then put them into a box and hid the box in the back of the closet. She even took all of Papa's clothes out of the laundry basket. That way, if the enemy soldiers came to the house, they wouldn't be able to find any men, not even any men's clothes, so they might think that the man who lived there had already been taken away.

Then Mama and Hansje waited. Hansje went outside and saw the bad soldiers push and pull some of his friends' daddies and uncles out of their houses and put them on the trucks. The Mamas and the little kids were all crying and trying to hold onto their husbands and daddies. Then, suddenly, the trucks were full, and they drove away.

Whew! Hansje and his Mama were so glad they were gone.

"Hansje," Mama said, "quick, fill the tea kettle about half full and put in on the living room heater."

Hansje ran to the kitchen and did what his Mama told him to do. He knew that when the kettle boiled the windows would steam up on the inside. That way, just in case some soldiers dressed as ordinary people walking by the windows would not be able to see if there were any men inside the house.

While the tea kettle was warming up, they ran to the back room, dragged that heavy dish cabinet away from the wall, rolled up the carpet again, and lifted the lid.

"It's okay, Papa!" Hansje shouted into the dark hole, "You can come out now. The bad soldiers have gone away."

So, Papa came out, and they had some lunch. But

from that time on, they always kept a kettle of water on the heater so the windows would stay steamed up.

After that, Papa never sat at the table, but always on the floor right underneath the window eating from a plate on his lap. That way, if someone peered in through a part of the window that didn't have steam on it, they wouldn't see Papa at all and would go away.

That's the way they lived for a long time. Every night Mama would read Hansje stories from the children's story Bible. Every night when he went to sleep, Hansje would pray that God would protect him and his family from the bad soldiers. And He did.

3 Hansje Gets a Haircut

When Hansje was a small boy, he didn't like getting his hair cut. He never did; even when he got older and was going to kindergarten, he hated going to the barber for a haircut. He had good reason to hate going to the barber because the barber was a bully who didn't like little kids. Even his name, Mr. Bullebak, sounded a bit like bully.

Once a month, ever since he started going to kindergarten, his Mama took him down the street, around the corner, and to the barbershop, right next to the cigar store. Hansje always complained, "I don't want to have a haircut. Please don't make me go," all the way there.

As soon as Hansje climbed into the chair and the barber put the white sheet around his neck and shoulders, the bullying would begin.

"Now sit still," the barber would say, snip-snipping his sharp scissors really close to little Hansje's face, "sit still, or I'll cut your ears off."

Hansje would hold still, as still as the bottles and boxes on the shelf in front of him, terrified of getting his ears cut off. He hardly dared to breathe. When bits of hair tickled his nose, he gritted his teeth and endured the tickling, knowing he couldn't move his hand to rub his nose.

He imagined what it would feel like to suddenly have a sharp pain on the side of his head, and feel warm blood running down the side of his neck, and hear the ear fall to the floor. He wondered what his friends in school would say when they saw he had only one ear.

He usually said a prayer before and after meals and when he went to bed, but when he was in the barber chair, he was so scared he hoped God wouldn't mind if he prayed right then. Hansje didn't move his lips but silently prayed a thought that God would protect him from those sharp snip-snipping scissors.

Getting a haircut didn't take long because Hansje didn't have much hair, but since he was small and very afraid, it seemed like a very long time. Later on, when he was eight or nine years old, he realized that Mr. Bullebak was probably joking and wouldn't actually cut off his ears. Then Hansje relaxed and, without moving his head, looked around the barbershop.

There were two things he looked at a lot. First were the mirrors on the wall: one huge mirror was on the wall in front of him, right above the shelf with the bottles on it, the other mirror was behind him. He could see himself in the chair and the barber beside him cutting his hair. But because the mirrors were slightly tipped, he could also see the back of his head and the back of the barber. Then, just above that reflection, he could see his front again, then above that the back. The reflections would go on and on until the edge of the mirror. He couldn't even count how many barbers the mirrors reflected.

The other interesting thing was the mysterious dark hole in the floor of the barbershop. While waiting for his turn, Hansje would see the barber finish the haircut he had been working on, take off the sheet, shake the hair off, grab the broom and sweep the hair into a square hole in the floor right near the wall.

Where did all that hair go? Hansje wondered. *How deep was that hole? What would happen if someone accidentally fell into that hole? Someone skinny and small like me? Would I disappear forever down there?*

Hansje had lots of questions but didn't dare ask any of them--not even when he was much older, like 12 years old, because he was still a little bit afraid of Mr. Bullebak snip-snipping his sharp scissors.

4 Hansje Gathers Firewood

When Hansje was five years old, he wished that he was older because he wanted to do things that big people did. His Papa and Mama were always talking about how they needed to find more food because their family was always hungry. And when it got cold they needed firewood to burn in the heater. He wanted to find things like that to help them, but he was just a little boy so, of course, he couldn't do anything to help. Or could he?

Sometimes his Mama would tell him about things he had never seen before, like candy, chocolate, sugar, butter, oranges, peanuts, and bananas. He had never tasted any of those things or even seen them because the bad soldiers had stolen all the ships and trucks that were used to bring those foods to his country.

Hansje always kept his eyes open when he wandered around the streets of his neighbourhood to see if he could find something valuable that didn't belong to anybody. One day he found some nails, a screw, and a long piece of string, so he brought them home to give to his parents. Another day he found an empty bottle to give to them.

His Mama and Papa were happy when he brought things like that home because they couldn't buy nails or string in stores anymore since the stores were empty. Hansje liked looking around for things he could bring home, not just because it made his parents happy, but because it made him feel like a grown-up and not just a little kid.

One day, Hansje did something that made his Mama very happy. It was a very cold month in winter, and they had only a little bit of wood and coal to burn in their heater to make the house warm and to cook their little bit of food on. When Hansje came home from playing outside, all his pockets were full of small pieces of firewood, and his arms were so full he couldn't open the door. He kicked the door until Mama opened it. Wow! She was so glad to see all that firewood! "We're going to be warm tonight!" she said happily. "Where did you get this firewood, Hansje?" she asked.

"Oh, I found it on the street," he said, not looking her in the eye. But that was only partly true. He did pick it up from the street, but he hadn't really found it. Instead, he had done a very dangerous thing to get it. If his Mama had known how he got all that firewood, she would have been worried and made him promise never to do it again.

But she didn't know, so the next day, Hansje took a cloth sack, folded it up flat and stuck it into his belt. He was only five, but he felt much bigger since he was doing something important for his whole family. He walked down the block to a certain street corner and hid behind a hedge with some other small boys. Then he waited.

He waited and waited until finally, he could hear the rumble of a large truck driving down the street. One enemy soldier was driving, and one was sitting beside him holding his big gun. The back of the truck was full of—you guessed it—little pieces of firewood! And sitting on top of the pile was a prisoner with a chain on his leg. The chain was fastened to the truck, so he couldn't jump off and run away. He was a good man who was from the city where Hansje lived. But the bad soldiers had taken him as a prisoner and made him work for them.

Hansje scrunched down further into the hedge so the bad soldiers in the cab of the truck wouldn't see him. His heart was pounding with excitement. He prayed that God would help him. Then he wondered if God would be okay with helping him do something sneaky.

As the big truck slowly drove by, Hansje crept out of his hiding-place. He ran right close behind the truck so the bad soldiers in the cab couldn't see him, not even in the truck mirrors. Other little boys jumped out from behind hedges and trees and joined Hansje behind the truck. As soon as the truck began to turn the corner, the prisoner started throwing armloads of firewood off the back of the truck.

All the boys picked up every scrap of wood that the prisoner threw off the truck. They could only do it by that corner because the road was so narrow that the driver had to be very careful how he drove and didn't have time to look in the rear-view mirrors.

What Hansje and those other boys did was, of course, a very dangerous thing to do. What if the bad soldiers had looked in their rear-view mirrors and had seen some boys picking up firewood from the street? They would have stopped the truck, jumped out, yelled at the boys, and shot their guns to scare them away. Also, the prisoner would get into big trouble. The boys knew this, so as soon as they had stuffed all the firewood into their bags, they quickly ran away home, and the prisoner just sat there looking as if nothing had happened.

Hansje got home, and his Mama was very happy with the bag of wood. That made Hansje happy too, and he felt even more like a grown-up. Hansje never told his Mama how he got that wood. Good thing too, or she would have been worried.

5 Hansje and the Reading Test

Hansje loved stories. Even when he was very small and couldn't read for himself, he loved stories. He loved to hear his Papa tell stories, especially on Sunday mornings, and he loved to hear Mama read stories to him from the big yellow children's Bible. It even had pictures, and Hansje loved to look at them, but he also looked at the pages with the words.

Even when he was just in kindergarten, he liked looking at words, and when Mama read from the children's Bible, she pointed at words like Moses, David, and Jesus, so that Hansje could learn them. No wonder he learned to read fast. He could hardly wait to read stories for himself. By the time he started grade one, he already knew all the letters and could read lots of short words. He couldn't write them very well, but he could read them. And after a few months, he could read very well.

One Saturday afternoon his grade one teacher came to visit Mama and Hansje at their house. It was like having a parent-teacher meeting, but in Holland, the parents stayed home, and the teacher rode her bicycle to the student's house to talk to the parents.

"Hansje is a bit bored in your grade one class," Mama explained, "because he can already read. He already knows all the letters and their names, and he gets bored when the class is reading only short phrases like 'the cat and the dog.'"

The teacher didn't believe her, so she took the beginning reader book out of her briefcase and gave it to Hansje and said, "Hansje, please read the first page of this book."

So Hansje opened the book to the first page and read the whole page and the next one and the next one, very fluently and very fast. No stumbling and wondering what some words were. The teacher still didn't believe that he was reading that fast.

His Mama has read this book to him so many times, he has memorized it, she thought.

So, she said, "Hansje, please read the book's last page; start from the end." She figured he couldn't have memorized the whole book and that he would stumble and read a lot slower from the last page where the boy and the girl in the story bring a puppy home to live with them.

Hansje turned to the last page, but he hadn't understood what the teacher meant when she said, "Read from the end." He thought she meant that he should read the last word in the last sentence, then back up through the whole sentence word for word to the first word of the sentence.

So, he read the last word, then the second last word, and so on. It sounded like this, "after ever happily lived all they and house their in girl the and boy the with live to came puppy The."

He read very fast without stumbling reading one sentence after another backward. Then the teacher laughed and said, "Stop, Hansje, that's not what I meant. But you don't have to read anymore. You already know how to read very well."

From then on, while the other kids were learning the shapes of the letters she let Hansje read all the story books he wanted, and he wasn't bored in that class anymore. He loved the reading class, except, of course, when the teacher made the class copy a page from their reader. Hansje hated doing that because he just could not write as neatly as the other kids. But he could read better than any of them!

6 Hansje Reads Exciting Books

Here's why Hansje liked reading books so much. Remember how some bad soldiers had come into Hansje's country and were stealing everything? Yes, it was a very bad time. Papas and mamas and uncles and aunties were scared of those soldiers. And, of course, so were all the boys and girls. It was a bad time in Hansje's country.

Hansje didn't like being cold in the winter, and hungry all the time, and afraid the bad soldiers would come into the house looking for things to steal, even looking for papas and uncles that might be hiding somewhere.

But there was one thing he could do to forget all that bad stuff, and that was to read stories about other times and other countries where there were no bad soldiers. Yes, he loved reading those kinds of stories. Stories about kids his age or a bit older living on a farm and helping to look after cows, pigs and chickens. And in those stories, there were always puppies and kittens to play with. Whenever he was reading, he was happy because it was like he was living somewhere else, and not in dark, cold, hungry Holland with scary soldiers walking around.

Some of you might be wondering why Hansje didn't watch funny programs on TV or listen to stories on the radio. Here is the simple answer. Nobody had even heard of television back in those days, and all the bad soldiers had stolen all the radios. But there were still lots of books.

Hansje also read the big yellow children's Bible. He knew all the stories already because Mama had read them to him before he knew how to read. But he read them anyway, especially the ones with big coloured pictures. One of his favourite stories was about Daniel because even though it was scary, he knew it would turn out good in the end. The picture that went with that story had Daniel standing in a cave looking up to the light of the opening way up high. And standing right alongside him was a fierce lion, with his mouth open. You could see his tongue and especially his long, sharp teeth. And behind Daniel and the lion were a dozen other lions, lying down or standing, there was hardly room for Daniel to stand.

The picture just made you want to read the story again and again.

Hansje also liked to read stories about other lands, especially lands that had volcanoes, warm water beaches, and palm trees with coconuts. He had never seen any of those things, of course, but he had looked at pictures and read the stories about them. One of his favourite countries was a country called Indonesia. It was much larger than Holland and had many big islands. Many people from Hansje's country had gone there in ships long ago and built cities and roads and started many farms. The people that had always lived on those islands in Indonesia couldn't read or write because there were no schools until the people from Holland built them.

Those schools needed teachers, of course, so more people had left Holland to go to Indonesia to teach in the schools, to work in the hospitals, and in the churches. They called those people missionaries.

What Hansje liked the most was the stories that the missionaries wrote back to their friends and family in Holland. The wrote about all sorts of adventures of traveling by boat from one island to another, or traveling on foot through the jungles, and climbing smoking volcanoes to look down inside and see the fire in them.

One time he read a story about a missionary who had gone into a hut to see a young boy the same age as Hansje whose Papa and Mama had died, so he was living with an uncle. But the uncle was a very bad man; he didn't love God and didn't treat his little nephew very nice at all. The boy was more like a slave than a nephew. Just as the missionary walked up to the hut, he heard a man yelling and then the sound of a stick hitting something, and right away a little boy started screaming and crying. It went on and on as the missionary ran around to the front of the hut.

There he saw a naked boy writhing on the ground with a big strong uncle standing over him and whacking him as hard as he could with a long thin bamboo stick. The missionary could see the red streaks all over the boy's body where the uncle was hitting him.

"Stop!" yelled the missionary running up to the uncle.

The uncle was so surprised to see the missionary he stopped beating his nephew. The missionary and the uncle talked for quite a while, and finally, the missionary took the boy by the hand and walked away to his house. There he and his wife looked after the welts and cuts on the boy's back and stomach and on his arms and legs. They washed him and put some clothes on him. And the next day they took him to an orphanage they had started where kind people would look after him.

That night as Hansje went to bed in his mind he could still see the drawing in the book, of the boy twisting and turning on the ground while his uncle was beating him. He could hardly imagine how much that boy must have been hurting. He had sometimes had a spanking with a carpet beater, and that hurt, but it was only on his behind, and he always had his pants on. He shivered when he thought of being hit over and over again on his bare skin. He couldn't sleep because of those thoughts.

So, he called Mama to come and bring him a drink of water. When Mama came with a small glass of water, she sat on the side of the bed and asked, 'What's the matter, Hansje?" So, he told her about the story he had read and about the picture he was remembering.

Mama was very smart and started talking to him about all kinds of other things that had nothing to do with beatings. They talked about other stories he had read. And she asked him questions about them to get his mind off his unpleasant thoughts. It worked.

Then towards the end, she asked him, "Hansje, when you grow up, what would you like to be? A fish salesman like Papa? Or a policeman like your Uncle Piet? Or a farmer with cows and horses? Or what?

Hansje thought for a while, and then he said, "Maybe I'll be a missionary."

"Well, maybe you will," Mama said as she kissed him good night again.

Mama went downstairs thinking how happy she would be if Hansje ever became a missionary. And Hansje closed his eyes and went right to sleep.

7 Hansje Keeps a Secret

Hansje was only five years old, and he wished that he wasn't just a little kid. He wanted to do things that were important, like help big people do the things they did. His Papa and Mama were always looking for things to eat, but he couldn't help them because he was still too little. Everyone else in the city was hungry too and looking for things to eat because of those bad soldiers who had come and had stolen all the food from all the stores.

One day Hansje's Papa had an idea. He went to the next-door neighbour who had a long back yard with several little sheds in it. They talked and planned to buy a small pig from a farmer they knew, put it in one of the sheds and feed it weeds, roots and even boiled grass until it was big and fat. Then they would kill it, butcher it, cook it, and eat it.

Of course, it was dangerous to be raising a pig in the city because the soldiers might hear about it and steal the pig. Also, after it was butchered, they might hear about it and steal the meat. So, Papa and the neighbour planned to feed it in the shed for about six or seven months until the pig was big and fat, then bonk it on the head to knock it out, and move it to the deep, cool cellar under the fish shop behind Hansje's house. Once it was down there, they could kill it, butcher the pig, and keep the meat cool.

There was only one problem. All the yards had big walls made of brick or wood that were way higher than a tall man's head. How were they going to move a big, fat, heavy pig from one yard to the other? They couldn't just walk out the neighbour's driveway onto the street carrying an unconscious pig between them and then turn into the driveway of Hansje's house. What if somebody saw them either from the street or some house across the street? They couldn't throw it over the wall either because someone might see them.

When Papa and the neighbour were thinking about this, they thought of Hansje. He could help them. Yes, even though he was very small, he could do something that would help them move the pig safely.

So, months later, after the pig was big and fat, the day came to move the pig. Papa and the neighbour didn't tell Hansje all about the pig because he was a very small boy and he might just forget that the pig was a secret and tell some of his little friends.

Here's what Papa said, "Hansje, the neighbour and I have to do a secret thing we don't want anyone to see, and you have to help us keep the secret. I want you to go and sit on the curb on the edge of the sidewalk, right between the two driveways. I want you to look up and down the street and at the houses across the street. If you see anybody by a window or walking down the street, you need to be quiet and just look at them. But when you don't see anyone, I want you to whistle a little song. Just whistle that funny song about the shark who got married. So, that's what your job is, whistle when there is no one, and it's safe, and be quiet when you see anyone. It's a grown-up secret, and you have to help us. Do you understand?"

Hansje nodded and said, "I keep quiet when there are people, but I whistle when there is no one around."

"Right, you got it!" Papa said.

Hansje walked to the street grinning a big grin because he could finally do something important and help adults keep a secret. He sat on the curb and was very quiet because two old ladies were slowly walking along the sidewalk. While he was waiting for them to go by, he whispered to God, "Please help Papa and the neighbour to do whatever they are doing." When they were finally gone, he started whistling that funny song about the shark who got married and all the crazy things the wedding guests did.

In the meantime, Papa and the neighbour quickly

went to the pig shed. While Papa was feeding some weeds to the pig, the neighbour who was a blacksmith and had very strong arms, stood behind the pig. He hit the pig on the top of its head, right between its ears, with a heavy hammer and knocked it unconscious.

Then Papa grabbed a foreleg and back leg; the blacksmith neighbour grabbed the other two legs, and, between them, they carried that heavy pig out of the shed and up to the wall between the two yards right in front of the workshop doors.

Hansje was quiet again because he saw two boys chasing each other down the street, but as soon as they were gone, he started whistling the funny song about the shark wedding again.

As soon as they heard Hansje whistling again, Papa and the neighbour swung the pig between them once, twice and the third time they let it go. Whoosh! Whump! It landed on the other side on the ground, right in front of the workshop door. Then Papa and the neighbour walked down the neighbour's driveway towards the street. Then they turned at the end, right behind where Hansje was sitting and walked along the other side of the wall up the other driveway acting as if nothing had happened.

When they got to where the pig lay, they quickly grabbed it by the legs again and carried it down to the cool cellar where they killed and butchered it. Hansje didn't see what was happening because Papa had told him to finish whistling his funny song about the shark eating all his wedding guests, and then go into the house and not come into the workshop.

That evening he was very happy to bow his head as Papa prayed to thank God for the boiled meat they were about to eat. Hansje didn't know what kind of meat it was or where it came from and he didn't care. He was hungry, and it tasted good.

Later, when he was seven years old, and all the bad soldiers had finally been chased away, his Papa and Mama told Hansje about the pig. If it hadn't been for that pig his whole family, including his cute, baby sister, Jannie, would probably have been very, very hungry and they would have gotten very, very skinny and maybe died.

Yes, they were bad times with those soldiers stealing all kinds of things. But Hansje was a happy little boy because he knew that while he was sitting on the curb, looking out for people and whistling when there weren't any, he was helping to keep a big people secret.

And even though he didn't know what the secret was about, it made him feel big, helpful, and more grown up, not just a little kid.

8 Hansje Plays the Stone Throwing Game

One day just before supper time, Hansje was playing a game with one of his friends called Wim. Naturally, it was a stone-throwing game because Hansje was a boy who loved throwing stones even though he knew it could be very dangerous.

To play the game Hansje and Wim each picked up a stone the size of a chicken egg and faced each other about ten steps apart. Hansje tossed the first stone at Wim, underhand, to land right in front of Wim so that he had to jump out of the way to keep the stone from bouncing on the ground and hitting him in the leg.

Then it was Wim's turn to toss his stone. Each time

they had a turn, they would back up a couple of steps. So after each one had several turns, they were quite a long way apart. Then they would start throwing overhand, and throw the stones way up high to land in front of the other boy.

Well, it was just before supper time and Hansje was playing this game, slowly backing his way towards his house, while his friend Wim was slowing backing his way towards his house across the street.

Hansje picked up a stone the size of a large marble, good for throwing a long way, and threw it as hard as he could towards Wim who was watching it fly. It landed quite close to Wim and bounced so high on the sidewalk; he jumped back with a yell.

Then it was Wim's turn to throw his stone. Hansje took a couple of steps back and watched Wim as he stooped down to pick up a stone. Then Hansje saw Wim swing his arm way back and just as he threw the stone, Hansje's Mama called, "Hansje, come in and wash your hands: it's time to eat."

"Yes, Mama," he hollered over his shoulder and turned back to look for the stone flying towards him. But he couldn't see it anywhere. He looked up in the sky, but couldn't see anything. So he thought Wim had just pretended to throw that stone.

He was just about to holler at Wim to hurry up and throw the stone for real when BAM!, a stone hit him right on the forehead.

Hansje was so stunned he didn't even yell; he just fell in a heap. Then, after a while, he slowly got up. His forehead hurt really bad. Everything around him seemed to be moving, even when he was standing still. And he also felt like he wanted to throw up. He stumbled into the house, and Mama said, "Hurry up and wash your hands. We are ready to eat." Then she looked at him and asked all kinds of questions. You know the way Mamas do when they are worried: "What's the matter? Why are you stumbling? How come you are so pale? What is that big bump on your forehead?

All Hansje said was, "Wim threw a stone at me, and it hit me on the head. It was an accident."

Which was true, of course. But what he didn't say was that they each had been throwing stones at each other. Do you know why he didn't say that? Because he knew he had disobeyed his Mama by throwing stones. And as he was coming in the back door, he saw, hanging on the wall, the carpet beater that Papa used to spank him with when he did something bad. So he didn't say anything about throwing stones.

He didn't feel a bit hungry. He laid down on his bed while Mama put cold cloths on his forehead, and he prayed that his head would stop hurting. He felt bad that he had disobeyed and played the stone throwing game. So he told God he was sorry he had disobeyed. Finally, he went to sleep.

He didn't throw stones much more that year because soon it was winter and Hansje and all his friends threw snowballs instead. And when spring came he learned how to make slingshots and was very happy, because a slingshot can make a stone fly much faster and farther than just throwing it.

9 Hansje and the Special Christmas Feast

The December that Hansje was six years old was not a fun time. First of all, it was much colder than usual. And the bad soldiers had stolen the gas, so no gas heaters worked, not even the gas burners in the kitchens. Everyone had to wear their coats all the time, even in the house. Not only was it cold, but there was also very little food to eat. Many days the stores had no bread, no milk, no meat, no food of any kind. The bad soldiers just kept taking food right from the farms and sent most of it away to their own country, so there wasn't enough left for the people in the country where Hansje lived.

When there was some food in the stores, people were allowed to buy just one or two things so that everyone would have a little before the food was all gone again. Even rich people couldn't buy all the food they wanted because that would mean other people would have nothing. Yes, during the time those bad soldiers were in Hansje's country, things were really awful.

One day, Hansje's Papa said, "I have a surprise! I bought some cheese, some special cheese called Slide cheese. We will have it for our Christmas feast."

Hansje thought he maybe remembered tasting cheese once long ago and liking it very much. He didn't know what a Christmas feast was, but it sounded so exciting he could hardly wait for Christmas.

On Christmas Eve Papa closed the curtains and lit the candles on the tiny Christmas tree. Hansje sat close to the coal heater with his parents who were holding his baby brother Wobbie and little sister Jannie on their laps. They sang Christmas carols while Wobbie and Jannie stared wide-eyed at the flickering candles. Hansje liked the carols, but his mind was more on what was coming next.

Then Mama put the little ones to bed and finally it was time for the long-awaited Slide cheese feast. She laid three small buns on top of the heater to warm up while Papa read the Christmas story from the Children's Bible. Hansje had heard the Christmas story before, and it was good, but smelling the toasting buns was even better.

When the buns were toasty and warm, Mama cut each one into two slices and put them on a plate on the small side table. Then Papa reached into his jacket pocket and pulled out a small, flat package and laid it on the plate, too.

Hansje could hardly wait, but first they folded their hands, closed their eyes, and Papa thanked God for the food and asked God to bless the special Christmas feast.

Then he took the flat package, opened it carefully, and there in his hand lay a piece of Slide cheese, just the right size to cover a slice of bun. He laid it carefully on one-half of a bun and said,

"Now watch me closely so you'll know how to eat this special Slide Cheese."

He held the bread and cheese to his nose and sniffed it. Hansje's mouth watered just watching him. Then Papa slowly and carefully put it into his mouth. But, just as the bun was passing his lips, his front teeth caught the edge of the cheese and slid it back. Then he took a bite, not of the cheese, just the bun. He chewed it with his eyes closed, obviously enjoying it a lot.

Next, it was Mama's turn. She did the same thing, sliding the cheese back and eating only a bit of bun. At last, it was Hansje's turn. Both Mama and Papa watched closely to make sure he did everything right. He sniffed the cheese, and its wonderful cheese smell reminded him of the last time he tasted cheese long ago. He slid the cheese back with his teeth, bit off a piece of bun, and chewed and tasted it for a long time with his eyes closed.

Then it was Papa's turn again. By the time they finally finished those six slices of buns, the candles had almost burned out, and when it was time for Hansje to go to bed, they still had the whole piece of Slide Cheese.

"Tomorrow is Christmas Day," he said, "and we will do this again. But then, when only three slices of the buns are left, do you know what we will do?"

"We'll cut the Slide cheese into three pieces and actually eat it!" Hansje shouted.

"Shush!" Mama whispered, "You'll wake the little ones."

"Yes," said Papa smiling at Hansje's excitement, "We'll eat the whole slice up tomorrow."

And that is what they did at their special Christmas feast.

It was the best Christmas feast Hansje could remember!

10 Hansje Brings Good News

In Holland, where Hansje grew up, everyone spoke the Dutch language. All his friends played together speaking Dutch, and his teachers taught in Dutch too. His Mama and Papa spoke Dutch as well.

But his Mama and Papa grew up in another part of Holland, called Friesland, where people spoke not only Dutch but also the Frisian language. So, his Mama and Papa could speak Frisian as well as Dutch.

When they moved to the part of Holland where Hansje was born, they spoke Dutch all the time, except when they were talking with each other and with all of Hansje's uncles and aunts since they all came from

Friesland, too, and spoke Frisian. That's why Hansje often heard them speak Frisian, telling funny stories and laughing. It made him wish he could understand Frisian.

They also spoke Frisian when they didn't want Hansje to know what they were talking about. Sometimes they were planning a surprise birthday party or talked about serious, grown-up things like some aunt having a baby, or bad things like sicknesses, or accidents, or what bad soldiers had done. Hansje would just sit there, listen and wouldn't understand a thing.

For many months, Hansje just sat quietly listening to his parents, and his aunts and uncles speaking in Frisian. It was a "big people" language, and that's why Hansje wished he could understand it. He very much wanted to do things big people did.

After a long time of listening to Papa and Mama speaking Frisian with his aunts and uncles, he realized that he was beginning to understand them. That's what happens when kids sit and listen to people talking another language and watch what they do. After a while, they begin to understand parts of it. They won't be able to speak it, but they can understand quite a bit. That's what happened to Hansje.

Now, Hansje was a very smart boy. He didn't want his Papa and Mama to know he could understand Frisian because then they would stop talking about interesting, big people things in front of him. So, as he got older he never let on that he could understand quite a bit of what his Papa and Mama were saying when they were talking Frisian.

When Hansje was about six years old, his Uncle Henk [rhymes with Hank] got terribly sick with fever and coughing. He was getting skinny, and felt very weak and had to stay in bed. He was married to Aunt Corrie who was Mama's sister.

After every supper time when Papa read something from the Bible, he prayed, and when Uncle Henk got so sick, he asked God to make him better.

Naturally, Mama wanted to help her sister, Corrie, look after her family. So every other day Mama got on her bike to ride out the town where Uncle Henk and Aunt Corrie lived, to cook meals, and clean up and help out wherever she could. Her other sister, Aunt Klaske [KLAHS-kuh] did the same thing on the days Mama didn't go.

Mama did that for many months. Sometimes she would come home and tell Papa how tired she was, and how rainy and cold it was getting with winter coming on. It was only about eight kilometres, and she could ride there in a little over half an hour, but it was still hard to do, especially if it was windy. She didn't want Hansje to know she was complaining, so she told Papa, talking in the Frisian language. But Hansje could understand almost everything she said, although he didn't let on he could.

Then one cold morning while Mama was getting dressed warmly to ride her bike out to Uncle Henk's house once more, the phone rang. The phone was in the kitchen where Hansje and Papa were finishing their breakfast. Hansje listened as Papa talked Frisian with Aunt Corrie. He understood enough to know he had some good news for Mama. So, while Papa was finishing the conversation, Hansje ran upstairs to tell Mama the good news.

"Mama, Mama," he said happily when he got upstairs, "You don't have to ride your bike to town anymore. Aunt Corrie just phoned Papa. You can stay home from now on because during the night Uncle Henk died."

Then a very strange thing happened.

Instead of smiling and being happy because she didn't have to go, Mama burst out crying and ran downstairs to hug Papa while Hansje followed slowly, completely confused and wondered what the problem was.

Didn't she hate riding her bike all the way out there in the cold rain? Hadn't she complained many times about how tired she was and how messy her own house was getting? Well then, why wasn't she happy she didn't have to do it anymore? Hansje just couldn't understand it at all.

Mama was crying, and Papa was talking soothingly to her, and Hansje just stood there in the kitchen, wondering what was going on. Sometimes this big people stuff was very confusing.

He looked at the clock and saw that it was time to go to school, so he put on his jacket, picked up the last piece of bread and cheese from his breakfast plate, and walked out the door, chewing his bread and cheese thoughtfully, as he walked to school. *I don't know what I did wrong,* he thought, *but I think I did something.*

11 Hansje and Papa Buy a Surprise for Mama

The bad soldiers were still in Hansje's country, but some of them were starting to run away. They had heard that a lot of good policeman and good soldiers were coming closer to chase them away. The bad soldiers were no longer stealing things, mostly because there wasn't anything left to steal, but also because the good soldiers had come in bomber airplanes and dropped big bombs on the railroad tracks, wrecking them so that no trains could run anymore. Without trains, they couldn't send the things they stole back to their own country.

This also meant that it was no use for the soldiers to grab young men and older boys to work in the fields and factories back in the soldiers' country. Without trains, they couldn't get them there. There weren't enough trucks and buses to move them either. So Hansje's Papa and his uncles and some other men started coming out from where they had been hiding and started living sort of normal lives again. Hansje's Papa even got his bike down from the attic hiding place where it had been for four years.

One day, Papa said to Hansje, "Do you want to go for a bike ride with me? We're going to a farmer to see if we can buy some vegetables."

Yes! Of course, he wanted to go! He got to sit on the back carrier and he hung onto Papa tightly. He didn't care where they were going; it was just fun being outside with Papa. Mama, too, was happy that their little son was going for a nice bike ride with his Papa, and maybe even bringing back some vegetables. But if Mama had known what was going to happen, she probably wouldn't have been so happy.

They rode out of the city along a long, straight, flat road in the country. There were mostly stumps and only a few trees alongside the road. People had cut them most of them down the winter before to burn them for warmth when it was really cold and to cook their food when the gas was off.

As they were riding along, Papa started to tell him what they were going to do. "Hansje," he said, "we're going to a farmer who is a good friend of our family. He has big gardens and grows lots of vegetables. But he also raises rabbits, and rabbits are good to eat. So, I hope he will sell us one to take home as a big surprise for Mama. She thinks we are only going for vegetables.

She will be so happy to get a rabbit."

Hansje was happy to hear that. He liked to eat meat, and it had been weeks, maybe months, since the last time he had tasted a piece of meat.

Suddenly they heard airplane engines, big ones flying down low, and smaller ones flying behind them, way up high. The moment Papa heard the planes he sped up his pedaling and went as fast as he could for about a half a block. There, just ahead was what he was looking for.

He jammed on his brakes; both Hansje and he hopped off the bike and jumped down into a long rectangular hole in the ground. It had a white post sticking up at each end so people could find it easily. It was about three feet wide, and five feet deep and about ten feet long. The bottom was muddy, but they didn't care. They crouched down in the bottom.

"The planes might drop bombs around here," Papa explained, "and when they explode the pieces will fly all over the place, but down here we are safe."

Hansje knew that already because he had learned that in Kindergarten. The teacher said, "When planes come over, bombs might fall, and when bombs hit the ground they explode; the pieces fly all over and hurt people or kill them. So get down on the floor and crawl under your desk, or when you are home, go down in the cellar."

Just like today's fire drills in school, so Hansje and his friends had planes-dropping-bombs drills in school. They called it an Air Raid drill. Hansje did have one little question to ask, "What happens if a bomb falls right into this hole?"

Papa just looked at him and said, "Well, what do you think?"

Hansje knew very well what would happen, but he really wanted Papa to say, "No bomb is going to fall into this hole. There are way too many other places for it to fall."

Instead, Papa explained a little more about what they were going to buy. "You are six years old, almost seven, and you like doing grown-up things, that's why I took you along. The bad soldiers will let us buy vegetables and bring them home to eat, but they don't let us buy meat. That is because they want the meat for themselves. But we are going to buy a rabbit anyway, hide it underneath the vegetables, and try to get past the soldier checkpoint going back into the city. When the soldier sees it is only a man and his boy with a box of vegetables, he might let us go by. But if it was just me, he might think I'm bringing something into the city that I'm not supposed to bring, so that's why I brought you along."

It sounded confusing to Hansje, but he didn't care, because he was excited to be with Papa and out in the country where he could clearly see the bombers. Papa was standing up and looking to where the planes were circling. He climbed out of the hole and pulled Hansje out too. Then he pointed way up ahead where big planes were dropping bombs on an airport. He couldn't see the bombs falling, but he could hear the Boom, Boom, BOOM of the exploding bombs in the distance. It sounded like far away thunder.

"Those planes have good soldiers in them," Papa explained. "They are dropping the bombs on the airport because the bad soldiers are there and trying to take off in their airplanes to fight against them."

He also saw little puffs of smoke where the planes were flying. "That is the bad soldiers shooting up at the planes," Papa said. "They have great big guns small shoot small bombs up into the air where they explode. If they explode close to an airplane, it will make holes in the plane, cause a fire, and the plane will crash."

Just then Hansje saw a puff of smoke right in front of a bomber. Right away the airplane started to slant downwards, trailing a long stream of black smoke. As he watched, he saw dark balls pop out from behind the plane. Under each of those dark shapes hung an even smaller black thing. He knew what they were because he had seen them before. Parachutes, of course! He counted them: 1, 2, 3, 4, 5. That was good. He didn't say anything out loud, but he thought, *Thank You, God.*

He had already learned in school that every bomber plane had a pilot, a co-pilot, a map reader, a bomb dropper, and a tail gunner. So when he saw five parachutes, he knew all five of the good soldiers were still alive and floated down to the ground, even though the big plane fell, burning and smoking until it smashed with a great thundering boom on the ground. He could see a tall column of smoke rising where it had smashed to the ground.

While all that was going on in the distance, Hansje

and his Papa got back on the bike and soon pedaled into a farm driveway. Papa started talking with the farmer, and Hansje walked around looking at the gardens and the barns.

Soon Papa called out, "Okay, let's go back!" On his bike front carrier, he had a big cardboard box filled with vegetables.

Away they went, happily biking along that long, straight road and getting close to the city. Suddenly a bad soldier stepped out from a shelter and pointed his gun at Hansje and his Papa. "Halt!" he shouted, which meant Stop!

Of course, Papa stopped, and Hansje jumped off the back of the bike.

"What's in the box?" the soldier shouted.

"Vegetables," Papa said.

"Open it," the soldier said.

So Papa opened the box, all you could see was cabbages and carrots.

But suddenly one of the carrots began to move, the soldier stuck the barrel of his gun into the box, and there was a rabbit! It was chomping on a carrot and sniffing the gun barrel.

Now Hansje knew they were in trouble. The bad soldier would leave the vegetables alone, but if he saw rabbits, chickens, pigs or anything else that was meat, he would take it.

Hansje just stood there with his eyes and mouth wide open. Inside his head, he thought about God and wondered if God would do something to help them. The soldier looked mean and pointed his gun at

THE MISADVENTURES OF HANSJE

Papa's stomach. Just as he opened his mouth to shout at them, Papa pulled three cigarettes out of his shirt pocket and held them up for the soldier to see.

"Would these cigarettes make the rabbit disappear?" he said.

"What rabbit?" the soldier asked as he took the cigarettes and turned away to walk back into the shelter.

Papa quickly closed the box, and he and Hansje jumped on the bike and took off with Papa pedaling as fast as he could. But Hansje had a question, "Why did the bad soldier just take the cigarettes instead of the rabbit?

"Because if he had taken the rabbit, it would have gone to the officers' kitchen, he wouldn't have had even one bite of it. But this way he had three cigarettes to enjoy all for himself."

When they got home, Mama asked, "So did you have a nice bike ride?

"Yes, we did!" Papa and Hansje both said at the same time.

Then Papa showed her the vegetables and also the rabbit. Was she ever surprised and happy to see that! Right away she and Hansje started cleaning and chopping vegetables while Papa went to the workshop to butcher the rabbit. They made rabbit stew and ate it for five days. Each time they ate a little more of it, they thanked God for that rabbit.

Mama never did hear about the airplanes and about the soldier who liked cigarettes. Papa didn't want to worry her, and neither did Hansje because he was a boy who liked to do big people things.

12 Hansje Cheers the Rescuers

"Hansje!" Papa shouted, "Come on. The liberators are coming. Let's go and see them. Today is our liberation day!" Hansje was only seven years old, and he had no idea what liberators were, but Papa sounded happy and excited, so he grabbed his jacket and ran to where Papa was waiting by the door.

Papa handed him a little Dutch flag with red, white and blue stripes and said, "Today we can wave our flag again. The good soldiers are coming, and the bad ones are all running away." Hansje waved his flag and saw that lots of houses had big flags on poles sticking out of windows and fastened to the roof. He had never, ever seen a single Dutch flag. Now he saw hundreds of them!

When they got to the big, central street, people were crowding along the curb. The bells in the huge St. Vitus church behind them were constantly ringing and ringing. Everywhere Hansje looked, people were laughing and smiling.

Papa was tall so that he could see easily from the sidewalk, but he pushed Hansje into the crowd to get to the front. Hansje squirmed and squeezed his thin body through the jostling crowd until he got a spot on the curb. The bright sunshine warmed his face, arms, and knees as he squinted into the light. He clutched his little flag, ready to wave, ready to shout, ready to sing a welcome to his rescuers.

He overheard two men behind him as they talked happily about the day. "It's Tuesday, May the 8th, 1945. Today is a day we'll never forget!"

Hansje heard the rumble of heavy army trucks up the street, and he heard the crowd there begin to cheer and sing. The noise grew louder until huge dusty-green trucks blocked out the sun. Shouting, laughing soldiers waved their machine guns from the backs of the trucks. The applause and cheers of the crowd around Hansje nearly drowned out the rest of the crowd's loud singing of the Dutch national anthem.

Soon tanks rumbled by them, pulling long-snouted cannons. Their thunderous booming had kept Hansje awake a few nights ago. Now those cannons seemed to be sniffing the air, eager to chase away the bad soldiers from the next city.

Suddenly the cheers died down as a column of prisoners, bad soldiers in their grey-green uniforms, shuffled past. Their pistol holsters flapped empty on their brown leather belts. They held their now-empty hands high or laced their fingers on top of their heads. Good soldiers, each with his machine gun ready to shoot, walked alongside them.

The crowd around Hansje stood silently watching the prisoners go by, but then they began to boo and hiss as a small group of the bad soldiers' officers came closer. Finally! No more strutting. No more snooty looks. No more shouting.

When Hansje saw them in their black officers' uniforms, he felt a twinge of fear. He had heard bad soldiers in black uniforms shout, "Shoot them! Shoot them dead!" And he had heard the guns shooting. But now nobody was afraid of them. Instead, people in the crowd rushed out and spat on them so much that their black uniforms were all slimy and yucky.

As the last truck in the parade rolled closer. Hansje cheered himself hoarse and waved his little flag at the good soldiers until one reached down, grabbed it, and waved it high as his truck rumbled on down the street. Hansje tasted the salt of tears, not because he lost his little flag, but for happiness at knowing the rescuers had arrived and that the bad soldiers would never make him afraid again.

As he turned to look for Papa, he realized he now knew what liberators were. And he knew exactly what he was going to thank God for in his bedtime prayer that night.

13 Hansje Loves Papa's Sunday Morning Stories

I just love Sundays, Hansje thought as he woke up one Sunday morning. It was still too early to get up, so he stayed in bed and stared at the ceiling.

Why do I love Sundays so much? He asked himself. To fill in the time, he thought of some reasons why.

First of all, I don't have to go to school. School is okay, but almost every day there is math, and that is not okay. In fact, that is awful. So, not having to go to school is one reason I love Sundays, he thought.

Other thoughts flitted through his head. *Going to Sunday school, that is usually pretty good. I like the Bible stories, the big maps of Bible lands, and I really like the large pictures of old fashioned, far away Bible lands and peoples.*

Sitting in church is a bit boring, but coming home is fun, listening to Papa and his uncles talking about all sorts of things as they walk home from church. Then at home listening to them talk and watching them smoke their cigars and drink their coffee, that is always fun.

And in the afternoon, there is lots of time to sit and read undisturbed, or in the summer go outside in the sun and sit there and read with no one to bother me.

But one of the best things about Sunday happened the very first thing after getting up. *And that is right now*, he thought, as he heard his Mama walk past his door on the way downstairs and to the kitchen. He hopped out of bed and walked quickly into his Papa and Mama's bedroom. Papa was already waiting for him, sitting up in bed with a big pillow behind his back. Hansje climbed onto the big bed and sat leaning against a big pillow right next to Papa.

They were waiting for Mama to make tea and bring it upstairs and there were always some small cookies on the saucer. But while they were waiting, there would be a story. Hansje wondered if it would be a story that Papa had heard from his Papa or some other older person.

He loved the stories that started, "Once upon a time, there was a young man who left home to go out to seek his fortune." The young man always met all kinds of interesting people as he was walking along and they joined him to seek their fortune too. Hansje didn't quite know what the fortune was that they were looking for, but they always ended up doing something very heroic like saving a princess, or catching some robbers, or fighting a dragon. And it always turned out really good for them in the end.

That was one kind of story, and Hansje liked them very much. But not as much as the stories about Papa and his brothers and the crazy tricks they pulled on each other. So, this morning, when Papa began to tell the story Hansje knew right away it would be a story about his uncles. Here's the story Papa told him that Sunday morning.

"When Uncle Leo and Uncle Bennie were just little boys in Kindergarten they came into the fish workshop where Uncle Teus [Tuys] and I were working with fresh herring, cleaning out the guts and cutting off the heads so we could fry them.

"Leo and Bennie stood on their tiptoes, looking at where we were working, with their eyes and noses just inches away from where we were cutting and cleaning the herring. They recognized the slimy guts, but some of the herring also had a long, finger-like lump of something that was pinkish orange and made up of what looked like very small round beads."

Hansje had seen those lots of times when he was cleaning herring, and he knew that they were eggs which the female herring would lay on the sea floor. Then the male herring would swim over them for a while, and after several days those eggs would turn into baby herring.

Just then Mama came with the tea, and they sat very carefully and still so as not to spill the hot tea. Hansje dipped his cookie into his tea, just a little bit and not too long or it would fall off into his tea, and that would be gross. After sipping their tea for a while and nibbling their cookies, Mama left to wake up Hansje's sister Jannie, and little brother Wobbie [rhymes with Robbie] and take them downstairs to get dressed and have breakfast. As soon as Mama left, Papa continued his story.

"What are those tiny round beads inside the herring?" Uncle Leo asked in his squeaky little boy voice.

"Those are seeds from which herring grow," I explained.

"Yes," Uncle Teus added, "Here, you can have some of these fish seeds and plant them in the garden the way you helped plant the carrot seeds last week."

"Just scratch a nice straight deep grove with a stick in a part of the garden that doesn't have any other plants growing in it," I told them, ""and then plant the seeds one at a time far enough apart, so the fish have room to grow."

"So little Leo and Bennie went away very happy that they were going to have fish growing in the garden. After about twenty minutes they came back.

'We planted them all,' Leo said, 'but nothing is happening.'

'Yeah, when are the fish going to start sprouting?' Bennie asked.

'Well, it takes a while for them to start sprouting,' I told them.

'Yeah,' Uncle Teus said, 'Why don't you go for a nice walk around the block, and maybe stop to play with some friends for a while, and then have another look.'

"So that's what they did. As soon as they walked off down the street, Teus and I grabbed a pail full of herring heads and ran to the garden. We saw where they had scratched a deep line and planted their herring seeds, so we stuck in a long row of herring heads. We stuck some quite a way in, with just their mouths out of the soil, others were up a little more, so the eyes showed. Then we went back to work.

"Sure enough, after about an hour Leo and Bennie came racing into the fish shop shouting,

'They're starting to come up! The herring are sprouting! We're going to have fish growing in our garden!'

"Yes, that's how we treated our little brothers. Fooling them all the time. No wonder they like playing tricks on people nowadays."

Hmm, Hansje thought, *maybe Uncle Leo and Uncle Benny are going to be here after church to drink coffee. If they are, I'm going ask them if they have planted any more herring seeds lately. Yes, I do like Sundays.*

14 Hansje Feeds the Fishes

"Hansje," Papa said, "we are going to Friesland during the two-week school vacation to have a big party. Do you know what we are going to celebrate?"

Hansje shook his head, then guessed, "A birthday?"

"No," Papa said, "Something much bigger and exciting than that. Your grandpa and grandma, Pake [Pah-kuh] and Beppe [Bep-puh], have been married for a whole forty years. So all Mama's sisters and brothers and their families are coming together to celebrate their fortieth wedding anniversary!"

Wow! Hansje had never been to Friesland, but he

had heard a lot about it from his Papa and Mama who were born there. He knew they spoke a different language there. Mama's Papa and Mama still lived there, that's why they were called Pake and Beppe because those were the names for Grandpa and Grandma in Frisian, the language everyone spoke in Friesland.

His grandparents in the city where he lived were called Opa and Oma because those are the Dutch words for Grandpa and Grandma.

Hansje had never met Pake and Beppe, and he had never celebrated a wedding anniversary, but he sure liked the idea of going on a trip and celebrating.

He had lots of uncles, aunts, and cousins in Friesland, too. But, even though he was already seven years old, he had never met any of them either. That was because, during the five years of war that had just ended a few months before, nobody was allowed to travel to other parts of the country. But now all the bad soldiers were gone, and only good soldiers were there. The grocery stores had food again, and things were much better.

When the day came for the journey, the whole family rode a bus to the harbor in a little seaside town. There they climbed into a small wooden fishing boat called a trawler. It was built to sail in shallow water near the coast, or on the inland sea called the Zuider Zee, which was also called Ijsselmeer Lake and was very shallow. Sailboats need to have a long wide plank called a keel that sticks down below the boat so that when the wind blows hard, they won't tip over. But a trawler doesn't have a keel sticking way down because then it couldn't go in shallow water, and also, a long keel might get tangled up in the fishing nets. Instead, it has a short, side keel board on each side of the boat to keep it from tipping over in a strong wind.

Papa loaded the suitcases into the fishing trawler, while Mama looked after Hansje's three-year-old sister Jannie and one-year-old brother Wobbie.

By the way, Jannie was named after her Beppe, that is, Mama's Mama who was called Janke in Frisian. Wobbie was named after his Pake who was Mama's Papa whose name was Wobbe [WOB-buh].

Mama helped Jannie climb down into the boat, Papa carried Wobbie, and Hansje looked after himself and had a great time clambering all over the fishing boat.

His great time didn't last very long, though. After they had left the shore, the winds started to blow hard, and the waves were really big, coming right up to the edge of the boat. The trawler was going up and down, UP and DOWN, UP and, well you get the idea. He didn't mind the UP part, but he really hated the feeling in his stomach during the DOWN part.

It didn't take very long before he suddenly had to lean over the edge of the boat and throw up all his breakfast. Papa laughed at him and said, "Hey Hansje, quit feeding the fish, they have enough to eat."

But Hansje didn't think that was funny at all. Mama wasn't feeling very good either and tried to find a place to lie down so she wouldn't throw up.

Hansje also laid down on some suitcases, closed

his eyes, and prayed that the trip would be over before he died from being so sick. As the trip went on and on, and he felt worse and worse, he felt like praying he would just die and get it over with.

After about two hours they got to a small island, called Urk. There they stopped and unloaded some things, then they started again, and Hansje felt like throwing up again for another hour.

Finally, they got to the harbor town of Lemmer which was on the shore of Friesland and the town where Papa had been born. Hansje was very glad, for two reasons. One was that the trip was finally over and the other was when he heard Mama say something to Papa in Frisian in a very stern voice, "We are not going back on a boat! We are going back by train!"

Hansje was glad to stand on dry land again, even though it felt like the ground was still moving under his feet. The whole family got on a bus with all their suitcases and rode for about an hour, making lots of stops along the way. At last, they got to Akkrum [AH-kruhm] where Hansje's Pake and Beppe and other relatives lived. When Hansje got off the bus, he felt great; he didn't feel like the ground was moving anymore. That night was the first time he ever thanked God for ground that didn't feel like it was moving!

15 Hansje Learns About Friesland

The minute Hansje walked into Pake and Beppe's house he smelled something strange. It was a smoky smell, not of tobacco like cigarettes or cigars; he knew that smell very well. And it wasn't smoke from wood or coal fires. It was something else.

Then he saw his Uncle Tommie put something into the burner of the wood burning cook stove. It wasn't wood, however, and it wasn't coal. He walked over to what he thought was the wood box and saw some strange looking bricks. They looked like they were made out of dried grass, or moss and twigs mixed and squeezed together.

"What are these bricks?" he asked Uncle Tommie, who was about ten years older than he was.

"These are bricks of peat," he said. "We call it turf and it is what we burn here in Friesland because we don't have wood or coal, but we have lots of dried up marshes where we can dig out this peat, dry it out and burn it."

So that is why the smoke smelled different. Once Hansje got used to it, he rather liked the smell. Also, Pake smoked a pipe whenever he sat down to relax in the living room. It smelled quite nice too, not stinky like Papa's cigarettes, more like his Sunday cigar.

Hansje hadn't been in his grandparents' house for more than fifteen minutes, and he had already learned something new. It wasn't the last thing he learned either.

He found out that Tommie loved to read and had a long shelf of books — all the books he had ever gotten in his life. That meant there were lots of books for Hansje to read. He knew exactly what he was going to do whenever there was nothing else going on — he would quietly slip upstairs to Uncle Tommie's room, sit in a corner and read adventure stories. He could hardly wait.

Hansje also noticed something else. After being on the fishing boat and the bus nearly all day, Hansje needed to go to the toilet. He asked an aunt where it was, but when he opened the door, she had pointed at and went in, all he saw was a bench with a hole in the top. No toilet and nothing to push or pull to make it flush. He peered down the hole. It was so dark he couldn't see anything, but he could sure smell something! Something stinky!

Well, he sat on the hole and did his job, then went out to look for his Uncle Tommie who knew everything about living in Friesland.

Hansje asked him about the toilet and Tommie explained. "Under that hole," he said, "There is a metal can, sort of like a large pail that catches all the nasty, smelly stuff. Then a couple of times a week a man comes along the back alley with a cart pulled by a horse. The cart is full of the same metal cans. He stops behind each house, right where each toilet is. He opens a small door, reaches in and pulls out the full toilet can, puts a lid on it, and lifts it onto his cart. Then he puts an empty can back under the hole, closes the small door, and goes to the next house. When the cart is full, he goes someplace special to dump all the cans and comes back with empty ones."

Hansje nodded to say that he understood, but he was thinking, *What if this man comes along with his cart just as I am sitting there on the hole? He might see my bare bottom!*

He not only thought about it then, but every time he went to the toilet and sat down, he hurried to get done as quick as he could, just in case the man and his cart would come by.

The next day some of his cousins came over to play since they were also enjoying their school vacation. Hansje loved to wander around the little town and play with toy boats in the canals along the meadows.

One day when they were playing hide and seek they heard some laughing and giggling from the other side of a thick hedge. Hansje and two of the cousins crawled on their bellies under the hedge to see what was happening on the other side. They saw three young soldiers sitting with three Frisian girls on their laps, and they were kissing them. So that's what the giggling was about!

Hansje and his cousins knew just what to do, even without talking about it. They slowly backed out of the hedge and quietly walked around the far side of the hedge to where the soldiers and their girls were.

As soon as they came into sight, the girls slid off the soldiers' laps and sat on the grass, all prim and proper, straightening their skirts and their hair. But the soldiers dug in their pockets and motioned for the boys to come closer. Then they held out some sticks of chewing gum, said something in English, and waved at the boys to go away. Hansje and his cousins eagerly took the chewing gum and scampered away. Yes, they knew what to do. All the soldiers in Holland and Friesland were good soldiers, from Canada, and they all had chewing gum.

During the next few days, other aunts and uncles arrived to celebrate the anniversary party. They went to a nice, sunny meadow, and everyone ate all sorts of goodies the aunts had made, like *fryske sukerbolle*, which is a kind of soft bread with little lumps of hard sugar and cinnamon in it, with lots of butter on top. It was delicious.

One aunt asked Hansje, "Do you want some *fryske dumkes?*" For a second Hansje was confused. He knew *dumkes* were little thumbs. But why was she offering him some little Frisian thumbs? Then she held out a plate, and he saw some small, hard cookies. He nodded, took some and found they tasted like anise and they had nuts in them, too. It was like a candy cookie. Yes, he liked *fryske dumkes* and ate as many as the aunts gave him.

Hansje also really liked the *droege woarst* which means dry sausage. It was really tasty because it was a mixture of meat and fish and had been smoked in wood and peat smoke.

And of course, there was plenty of lemonade for Hansje and his cousins to drink. Some of Hansje's uncles liked to sip *beerenburg* which is a mixture of nasty tasting *jenever*, meaning gin. with more than a dozen different kinds of herbs mixed into it.

At the end of the celebration, a photographer arrived and set up his camera on its stand. He got everyone arranged by families, with Pake and Beppe sitting on nice chairs in the front and centre, underneath a cardboard crown that said, *40 jier hecht oaneinsmeid,* which means "40 years tightly welded together."

The actual words for *welded* meant they were like two pieces of iron heated white hot by a blacksmith and then pounded together with a large hammer until they become one piece. That was a pretty good picture of their marriage. Pake and Beppe were the very oldest people that Hansje knew; he couldn't imagine anyone being that old, and to be married for a whole forty years. That was almost six times as long as he had lived! He thought about Papa and Mama who were married only eight years. He hoped that they would stay together for forty years too. When he thought about it, he hoped that God would let his Papa and Mama live long enough so that they could celebrate like this too.

16 Hansje Rows a Boat

One day, when Hansje was sitting on his bed in Uncle Tommie's room, reading his books, his uncle came in and said, "Hey, do you want to go for a walk and row a boat?"

Well, of course, Hansje wanted to go. He liked reading his uncle's books, but he also wanted to go and row a boat on a canal or a river. At least it wouldn't be going UP and DOWN, and UP and DOWN, making him sick like that trip on the fishing trawler had done.

They didn't have to walk very far, just down to the end of their street, across a meadow, and to a wide canal. There, tied to a post, was a rowboat. Hansje had never been in a rowboat before. He knew how to swim a little because since the end of the war he had been going to the swimming pool every Saturday afternoon and learned to swim there.

Tommie and Hansje got into the rowboat, and Tommie untied the rope from the post, then sat down in the middle seat and started rowing.

The ride was great. The boat wiggled quite a bit when Hansje got in, but it was so nice and smooth when Tommie rowed, not at all like those nasty hours going UP and DOWN in that fishing boat a few days before.

It was fun to sit there in the back of the rowboat and talk with Tommie as he rowed along the canal. It was so quiet and peaceful. Hansje saw frogs, ducks and other water birds that didn't even fly away when they floated by. After a while, Tommie asked, "Do you want to row a while?"

"Yes!" Hansje exclaimed.

Very carefully, without standing up, they changed seats. Hansje took hold of the oars and began to row. At first, he splashed quite a bit, but eventually, he learned to push down when he pushed the oar handles forward and pull up when he pulled them back. Then it went pretty well. Once in a while, he got sort of close to the shore, and he learned to steer by pulling harder on one oar than on the other one.

When they got to a nice, shady place, Tommie said, "Let's stop here and eat a little lunch." Hansje was very happy to hear that because with all that rowing he had become quite hungry and wondered about lunch time.

He rowed under some big trees and bumped the front of the rowboat into the shore. Tommie climbed past him, stepped onto shore, pulled the rope tight and tied it to a tree so that Hansje could get out.

As Hansje was putting the oars down inside the rowboat, he noticed that right by the handles someone had carved something. On one oar it said "*ORA,* " and on the other oar it said "*LABORA.*" So while they were sitting under a tree eating their *sukerbole* and cheese, Hansje asked Tommie, "What is that writing on the oars about? I don't understand it. Is it Frisian?"

"No," he said, "those are Latin words. The one that says *ORA* means *Pray*, and the one that says *LABORA* means *Work*. What would happen if you only used one oar to row?"

Hansje knew the answer to that because he had accidentally pulled hard on one oar, and just sort of let the other one float. "You go around in circles and don't get anywhere," he said.

"Right, if you only work hard but don't pray to God, you don't get what you need. In the same way, if you only pray hard but don't work, you also don't get what you need. You have to do both: *Pray* to God to give you what you need, and *Work* so that you get it."

It seemed like a very good idea to Hansje, and he wondered if it would work to get his own boy-sized bike. He could already ride Mama's bike by standing up and riding the pedals without sitting on the seat. But, of course, he couldn't ride Papa's bike very well since it had the cross bar and he could only ride it by putting one leg under the crossbar, and that was hard, and dangerous too. He had seen some of his friends with their knees skinned from falling while trying to ride their fathers' bikes. He sure didn't want that to happen to him.

After more than a week in Friesland, Hansje's family returned to their hometown, but *not* by fishing boat. Oh no, Mama didn't want to get seasick again, so they went back by train. It cost more money, but it was much faster. It only took about two hours, and they were home — without any puking — which made Hansje very happy.

And what was even more exciting, the following year he got a bike of his own. Yes, his very own boy-sized bike! He had prayed for it lots of times when he went to sleep at night, but he hadn't done much work. That work came later. He started delivering parcels for his Papa's store, and he did that for years and years until he was twelve years old and they left for Canada.

17 Hansje Rides in a Truck of Terror

Poor Hansje was down on his knees and elbows, his hands clasped in prayer, his eyes tightly shut, and his lips were whispering, "Help me. Please help me. Help me." The frozen steel floor of the army truck sucked the warmth from his knees and forearms. His seven-year-old body shivered as much from cold as from fear.

Hansje was not alone; the truck was packed with several dozen other children about his age. But while he was crying and praying desperately, they were happy, excited, laughing, talking and singing. Why was Hansje the only one who was terrified, down on the floor, praying anxiously for help—help that didn't come? What was happening?

Hansje's Mama had told him many, many times, "Don't ever get into a car or on a truck that is driven by someone you don't know." But this time, his Mama was the very person who insisted that he climb on that truck. Hansje had shouted, "No, no! I don't want to go!"

But she sternly said, "Don't be so silly, Hansje." And when a big soldier with the word *Canada* on his uniform picked him up and lifted him onto the back of the truck, she had smiled at the soldier.

Hansje couldn't understand it. He was so confused. He kept praying, "Help me. Help me." But instead of help, a smiling soldier slammed the end gate shut, the diesel motor rumbled and roared to life, and with a jerk and a tooting of the horn, they were traveling down the street, away from Hansje's home and out of his neighbourhood—no help, no hope.

After a while, the truck stopped. Hansje stood up and jumped down to the ground with the other children. He looked around; there were other army trucks and lots more children jumping out. Then he saw the building beyond the trucks and suddenly a wave of relief flooded over him. It was the KRO radio station studio. He had been there before. It was only a few blocks from his neighbourhood. He wiped away his tears. He knew where he was. He was safe.

He followed the crowd of excited children into the

building and sat with hundreds of others in the huge auditorium, looking down on the brightly lit stage.

A man walked to the microphone on the stage and said, "Today is December the 5th, the first Sinterklaas [SIN-ter-klahs] day since the end of the war. Sinterklaas is on his way. He will soon be with us. Let's sing to welcome him!"

Hansje loudly sang the Dutch Santa Claus songs along with all the other kids, all his fears forgotten.

Zie, ginds komt de stoomboot uit Spanje weer aan.
Hij brengt on St. Nicholaas, ik zie hem al staan.

"Look, there is the steamship coming from Spain;

It brings us, St. Nicholas, I can see him standing there."

After a few more Sinterklaas songs, the tall, white-bearded saint strode onto the stage to much applause and shouting by Hansje and the other kids. He wore his bishop's red and gold robes, a tall, red hat with a gold cross on his head, and he held a golden staff in hand. His black servant, Zwarte Piet [ZWAR-tuh-Pete] followed him.

After more singing, every child received a bag of candy and a small present. What a party! And then, it was all over. Hansje was tired but happy.

But as the kids crowded around the trucks, he started to be afraid again. *What if he got on the wrong truck? What if they made him get out at the wrong place?*

Hansje had had enough of trucks. He sidled quietly to the edge of the crowd. He crossed the sidewalk, then darted across the main road, and jogged towards his neighbourhood. He passed the hedges where, two years ago, he had hidden while he waited for the German firewood truck. Then he saw the corner to his street. A few minutes later he was home. Safe at home, and with candy.

That night Hansje added a line to his bedtime prayer, "And thank you for keeping me safe on that truck. Amen."

18 Hansje Goes on an Unforgettable Holiday

One day, when Hansje was eight years old, Papa said to him, "Hansje, during this summer vacation we are going on a whole week's holidays."

"What are holidays?" Hansje asked. He had a holiday in his whole life. He went to school on weekdays, and to church on Sunday, and he helped Papa in his fish store, butchering fish, or cleaning up afterward. During his two-week-long summer vacation, he just helped Papa most of the days. He didn't know what holidays were, but they sounded good.

"Mama and I, you, your sister Jannie and your

little brother Wobbie are going to Limburg. You will climb hills, see valleys, and even go into caves."

Hansje was very excited because he lived where the land was flat and grassy with trees and houses, and he had never seen a hill except in pictures. Then Papa explained they would also take along an uncle and aunt.

"We're all going in our little cargo van and drive nearly all day to get there." He also told Hansje that they were going to stay on a guest farm and drive and walk and look all over that part of the country for a whole week and then drive back all day to get home.

Wow, Hansje could hardly wait! He wanted to climb into the back of the van right away. Except for that trip to Friesland the year before, he had been outside of his own town only a few times. But on this trip, there would even be caves. He hoped they would be dark, scary ones.

That little cargo van was not at all like a regular six-passenger van. First of all, it was a lot smaller. Second, there were no doors on the sides of the back of the van, just a door in the back with a little window in it. Third, there were no seats, so all the passengers had to sit or lie on suitcases, pillows, and blankets like you would have to do in a pickup truck. And fourth, there were no windows in the sides of the van at all. So nobody in the back could see anything outside except if they peered through the little window in the back door to see where they had been.

Oh, and one more thing, the doors on the driver's side and the passenger side did not have hinges at the front like all cars have now. Instead, they had hinges at the back and handles at the front. That meant when you opened the door it was easy to get in and get out. It also meant that you could never open the door when the van was moving because the wind would catch it and it would fly wide open.

Of course, no one should ever open a door in any car when it is moving, but at least today's cars have hinges at the front so that if someone does open the door when the car is moving, the wind will try to close it again.

Finally, the day came. Early in the morning, they piled all their stuff into the back. The aunt and the uncle climbed into the small back end of the van and got themselves comfortable, then Hansje and Jannie climbed in. Papa closed the back door, and he got in the front to drive. Mama sat next to him with little two-year-old Wobbie on her lap. This was before they invented seat belts and car seats for little kids, so they just sat there.

Mama grabbed the door handle and slammed her door hard to shut it properly. There was something wrong with the lock; that's why she had to slam it so hard. Then the trip started. It wasn't that far to that farm in Limburg. But the roads were very narrow, and every ten minutes they had to go through a town, so it was a really, long time for four people to sit in the dark and in the back of that tiny little van. But they stopped to go to the bathroom quite a few times, have a drink of water and some sandwiches, and finally, late in the afternoon, they got there.

The farm people in Limburg talked somewhat funny, a different kind of language, but Hansje and his parents could sort of understand it. They had made mattresses out of bundles of straw and laid them all in a long row in a big stone barn. Everything was very clean and smelled very nice like hay and straw. There were dozens of other people sleeping there too. It was something like a campground with everyone sleeping in the same huge room. Most of the people just slept in their clothes with a blanket over them.

The next morning, they went to all sorts of different places to see things that Hansje had never seen before. They climbed high up on a hill and saw a panorama, where you can see far away because you are high up. Hansje had never been able to see any farther than the far end of the street, or maybe across a big playground or piece of pasture. He got dizzy from looking so hard at things so far away.

Then, on another day they went into the caves. They called them catacombs. Deep, long tunnels into the ground where everything was very dark, damp, and mysterious, and very scary when somebody dropped the only flashlight which went out for a while. Hansje walked for a long way, always making sure he was holding Papa's hand, or his uncle's, because he didn't want to get lost in one of those cave tunnels under the ground. He didn't understand everything the guide was saying, but it was something about long ago people hiding and living down there because they loved God and read the Bible, but there were very bad people in the country who wanted to take away their Bibles and burn them and punish the people who read them.

Then on another day, he had a kind of lemonade that he had never had in his life before. It was called Prickle Lemonade. He thought it was the very best thing he had ever drunk in his whole life! It was just ordinary lemon soda pop, but it was the very first soda pop he had ever had, so he thought it was great.

They also visited a castle called Valkenburg [FALL-ken-burg] that had been built nearly 1,000 years before, and some soldiers attacked and wrecked some of it about 600 years later. Hansje just loved vacation and holidays, but, too soon, it was time to go back home.

One morning they packed up their pillows, blankets, and suitcases and stacked them all back into the little van. Then the four climbed into the back and Papa closed the door. Mama took Wobbie on her lap and reached out to close the door with a slam.

But just before she slammed the door, the farmer's wife came up to say goodbye in her funny language. Mama and the farmer's wife talked for a while, then the farmer's wife closed the door for Mama, but not with a slam. Mama was too polite to open the door again and slam it hard while the farmer's wife was still standing there waving goodbye to them. So she thought, *I'll wait until we are around the corner and then I will slam the door, so it is properly shut.*

But instead of remembering, she forgot. It was probably all Wobbie's fault because he was waving his new red shovel about and nearly hit Papa in the face with it while he was driving around the corner. You can imagine what would have happened if he had. So Mama fussed with Wobbie and made him put his little shovel down near the floor and away they went, while she forgot all about slamming the door to make sure it was really latched shut.

Everything went well until about an hour later when they were going down the last big hill in Limburg, and at the corner, there was a bend to the left. When a car makes a sharp left turn, the passengers always slide to the right, sometimes leaning against the door.

Suddenly, Hansje heard a terrible BANG!!! on the right side of the van. It sounded like a car or bike had run into the side of the van. At the same time, Papa slammed on the brakes hard, and everybody in the back slid, Wham! up to the front of the van. Then Hansje heard his Papa open his door and jump out of the van. In the meantime, his uncle was kicking and pounding at the back door and shouting, "Open the door! Open the door!"

Papa yanked the back door open, the uncle jumped out, and then the rest of them climbed out. Hansje saw right away what the trouble was. The door on the passenger side, the one that Mama had forgotten to slam shut, had suddenly flown open when she leaned against it as they were going around the corner to the left.

With the hinges at the back instead of the front, the door had instantly opened all the way and slammed against the side of the van. Of course, his Mama and his little brother Wobbie had fallen out at full speed, landed on the gravel, slid and rolled along the side of the road.

He saw Wobbie sitting in some gravel on the side of the road. He was crying and bleeding from little cuts on his arms and head, and he had also peed his little pants. With tears and blood and pee, he was a wet, messy little boy. And he was screaming at the top of his lungs, "My shovel! My shovel! My shovel!"

So the first thing Hansje did was to look for his little red shovel. He found it under the car; it was a little bent and scraped, but it was still okay. So he bent it straight and gave it back to his little brother. Right away he quit screaming and started digging in the gravel at the side of the road. Hansje ran to where Papa, the uncle, and the aunt were looking for Hansje's Mama.

They had a hard time finding her because there were all kinds of prickly thorn bushes on the side of the road. She had tumbled and slid in among them somewhere, but they couldn't see her.

Suddenly, Hansje saw her shoes sticking out between two big concrete posts. He yelled, and everyone ran over to see. Sure enough, there was Mama, upside down in a deep ditch filled with barbed wire and prickly thorn bushes. Papa grabbed one leg, his uncle grabbed the other leg, and they both pulled and pulled. Finally, they got her out and laid her on the road. She was lying quietly, looking like she was sleeping.

Hansje ran over to see, and so did Jannie, who had

been looking after Wobbie, but their aunt grabbed them and tried to hold their faces against her tummy so they couldn't see their Mama like that. But Hansje had already seen a lot and jerked away from his aunt to see some more.

Mama was bloody everywhere. The gravel had scraped lots of skin off one leg. Her shoulder and arm on one side were scraped and ripped, and her face was cut in lots of places. After a few minutes, her eyes fluttered open, and she started to moan and cry with pain.

When another car came by, they put Mama and Wobbie into it. Then Papa and the aunt got in. They drove off to go to a doctor's house. Hansje and his sister Jannie and the uncle were left to wait by the van. They waited nearly all day. While they were waiting, Hansje kept walking away to look at the part of the ditch where they had pulled his Mama out. As he stood with his back to the rest, he closed his eyes and prayed for his Mama.

Finally, his Papa came back to get them and the van. By that time, the uncle had fixed the brake pedal on the van. Papa had stepped on the brake so hard; he had bent the pedal. They drove to the doctor's house, carried his Mama out, and put her in the back of the van so she could lie down. Then Hansje, Wobbie, and Jannie sat in the front with their Papa while the aunt and the uncle looked after Mama in the back. Papa drove all the rest of the night to get home. He drove very gently, not going over any bumps. Also, they tied the door handle with a rope to the steering post inside of the car so the door wouldn't open again.

When they finally came home, they made a bed in the living room for Mama, and she lay there for nearly two weeks. Every day a doctor or a nurse came by, checked on her, and changed all the many, many bandages. The long, deep scrape on her leg was the last to be healed. But finally, she could walk again.

Meanwhile, Papa put a little slide lock on the inside of that door, and after that, whenever Hansje would ride with his Papa, his Mama would come running out of the house shouting, "Remember the slide lock! Remember the slide lock!"

All this happened long ago, but even after Mama became a Grandma and her grandkids called her Beppe, they could still see the little scars on her face. Sometimes, when Hansje saw those little scars, he thanked God for answering his prayer for her.

19 Hansje Makes a Conker

Hansje loved to play with other boys. Sometimes they played games like hide-and-seek, or tag, or marbles. And sometimes they played with conkers. Conkers are the nuts inside the horse chestnuts that fell from the trees in the fall. When they fall from the trees, they are about the size of an apple. But you sure wouldn't want to catch one with your bare hands when it fell! No, instead of being nice, smooth, and reddish, horse chestnuts have prickly spines sticking out all over them and are greenish yellow.

You can pick them up, carefully keeping your fingers between the spines and carry them home in a box or bag. If someone was acting crazy and threw one at you, you had better duck out of the way because if it hit you on bare skin or against a thin shirt, the spines would pierce right through your skin. To get at the seed you have to cut the ugly, thick, greenish-yellow spiky skin part off, and Wow! There is the seed — a beautiful, shiny brown conker, the size and shape of a slightly flattened golf ball.

One game Hansje played with conkers was to make a hole through one and tie it on the end of a string. Each of his friends also made a conker on the end of a string; then they tried to break the other person's conker by taking turns and whacking it with their conker.

Another game was to string about ten or twenty conkers on a long, thin piece of rope like giant beads and make necklaces or belts. Hansje also made a horse's bridle with about thirty conkers which he looped over the neck, shoulders, and under the armpits of a friend who would pretend to be a horse running ahead of Hansje who was holding the ends of the conker bridle.

When Hansje was very small Papa always bored the holes through the conkers for him. But when Hansje was in grade three, he wanted to do it himself. So he got a screwdriver with a small thin end and, holding the conker in the palm of his left hand, he pushed and twisted the sharp screwdriver into the conker. It worked well. Hansje had strong hands and wrists. He drilled in deeper and deeper.

Then suddenly the sharp screwdriver poked all the way through the conker on the other side. But it didn't stop there — it went right through the skin on the palm of Hansje's left hand, through the flesh, and then almost out through the skin on the other side.

Hansje was very surprised and let out a yell of shock and pain. He was holding out his hand with the screwdriver and conker dangling from it. The sharp end of the screwdriver had gone so far into his hand it pushed up the skin on the back of his hand, so it made a little pyramid.

When Hansje saw that, he started crying really loud; and Mama came running up and pulled the screwdriver and the conker out of his hand. Then she held it under the cold water tap to rinse the blood that was pouring out. It finally stopped bleeding, and Mama put iodine medicine and a bandage on the inside of his hand. The iodine stung and hurt much worse than the screwdriver had in the first place.

Papa came in and showed Hansje how to hold a conker tightly between his thumb and forefinger, not in the palm of his hand. But Hansje decided he would wait until he was in grade four before he tried boring holes in conkers again.

A few months later, it was Easter week, and his family was reading the story of how Jesus was nailed to a cross. Hansje couldn't help looking at the little scar on the palm of his left hand. He remembered that the little sharp screwdriver had hurt a lot and tried to imagine how much more it would have hurt Jesus when He voluntarily held out his hands and the soldiers pounded big, rusty spikes right through both his hands and his feet.

20 Hansje and His Push Cart

When Hansje was eight years old, he wanted a bicycle just like Papa and Mama had. He wanted a bike so he could go fast, much faster than he could run. But Hansje's Mama didn't want him to have a bike. She thought he would go way too fast on it, and probably hit a car and get hurt. But Mama was wrong. He didn't go fast on a bike, and he didn't hit a car, but he still got hurt.

Hansje's friends, Wim, Arnold, Hennie, and the others all wanted bikes, too, and since no one gave them bikes, they had to invent something else. They went to a junkyard where people dumped broken things they didn't want anymore. There they found some old bike wheels without tires. Some wheels had spokes in them, and some just had the rims. When Hansje and his friends saw those wheels, they got a couple of ideas.

Their first idea was to use the bike wheels that didn't have any spokes in them as hoops. Hansje and his friends each took one and used the hoops to have races up and down the street to see who could run the fastest, rolling his hoop ahead of him while whacking it with a small stick. They were very good at it and had all kinds of racing games with the hoops. Hansje's Mama saw him running up and down the street rolling his hoop, and she called out to him, "Not so fast, Hansje! You'll hit a car, and get hurt."

Hansje slowed down for maybe half a minute. But then he started running again. After a couple of weeks, Hansje and his friends got tired of that game and decided to invent something else. Hansje's Mama was happy they stopped racing up and down the streets, but if she had known what would happen after a couple of weeks, she would not have been at all happy.

The boys went to the junk yard again and found some old bike wheels with the little center part called the axle and the spokes still in them. They also found bolts that would fit into the axle holes. Then they found some old wooden boxes and asked their older brothers or papas to help them fasten the wheels onto the boxes.

Hansje's Papa had a fish butcher store behind their house. A man whose name was Jaap [YAHP] worked in that store. One day, during lunch time, Jaap helped Hansje put two wheels on his wooden box, and he also made a wooden push handle so he could push his cart.

Hansje was very happy with his pushcart. What he liked the most was that, without tires, it made a lot of noise when he ran pushing it up and down the street.

To make it even more fun, Hansje put some stones in the bottom of his box, some empty tin cans, and some pieces of metal junk. Also, when he pushed his pushcart, he deliberately steered it through all the potholes and hit all the rough parts of the road so that everything in his pushcart rattled and clattered, making a terrible racket. Right away, all Hansje's friends put noisy, rattling junk in their pushcarts, too.

Then, of course, Hansje and his friends had cart races to see who could push their cart down the street the fastest. When five boys pushed five wooden push carts with bare rims and no tires down the street, with all the loose rocks and cans rattling inside, it made a terrible racket. Dogs barked, babies cried, and mamas ran out into the front yards of their houses to see what was going on. Hansje and his friends loved making noise and scaring the neighborhood. They went everywhere with their pushcarts. They played with them after school for many weeks.

Then one day it rained nearly all day. Winter was coming soon, and they knew they wouldn't be able to push their carts when it was snowy. Besides they would be busy skating and pulling sleds. Late that afternoon, Hansje pushed his cart over to his friend Arnold's house right across the street from his own house and played there for a while.

Suddenly he heard a special whistle. It was Papa, whistling for him to come. He knew it meant he had to stop whatever he was doing and go home right away because Mama was putting supper on the table.

So Hansje turned his pushcart around and ran as fast as he could down the gravel driveway, and bumped across the sidewalk, and zipped across the street without even looking and WHUMP!!!! CRASH!! BONK!!

Yes, it had happened.

No, it wasn't a car. It was a motorcycle. All that Hansje saw was something big and blue and the next thing he knew there was the WHUMP!!!! CRASH!! His head hit the pavement. That was the BONK!! Then he knew nothing for quite a while.

When he finally opened his eyes, everything was quiet, but there were lots of people around. Mama was by his side, and Papa was running across the street leaving the door of the store wide open. Papa helped Hansje sit up, and he saw a man looking angrily at his bent and broken motorcycle lying on its side on the wet street.

Hansje's left hand was very sore. He looked at it and saw that his thumb was all bloody and didn't have any nail on it anymore. The push cart handle had hit his thumbnail so hard; it ripped it right off. You can imagine how much that hurt. But, the worst of it was when Hansje finally stood up and looked for his pushcart. It had disappeared! It was like magic.

One minute he was a boy happily racing his

pushcart home for supper, the next, he was a very sad boy with a sore and bleeding thumb, a big bump on his head, and no pushcart. It had turned into small pieces of kindling, one bent wheel lay underneath the motorcycle, and the other wheel far down the street.

He had to go to the doctor to get a special bandage put on his thumb. It stuck up for many weeks and hurt every time he touched it against something before finally, another nail started to grow. Another very sad thing was that by the time his thumb got better, the snow had started to fall, and the time for push carts was past. He never pushed a cart again until he was a big man. Then he pushed a baby carriage with a cute baby girl inside it whose name was Valorie.

That night, when he lay in bed, he said his regular little prayer poem and then had a happy thought. He didn't know how to pray about that happy thought, so he didn't say anything to God, but he thought a very thankful thought, like this,

I'm so happy that Papa and Mama felt so sorry for me for having hurt my thumb so badly, and for wrecking my push cart that they didn't give me the spanking with the carpet beater that I deserved for running across the street without looking, which no one is ever supposed to do. It was sort of like a prayer, so at the end, he softly said, "Amen."

21 Hansje is Embarrassed at School

Hansje loved books and reading. He started liking books when he was barely able to walk or talk and Mama read to him while he looked at the pictures. It seemed that even in Kindergarten he was already reading a little.

He loved reading the stories in school books and what he loved the most was when the teacher read a chapter from a book out loud to the class. When he was nine years old and in grade four, the teacher read about a boy and a girl who lived on a farm. Their names were Jaap and Gerdientje [ger-DEEN-tjuh]. They helped in every part of the farming—looking after animals, sowing and reaping the grain, all kinds of things—and they had a lot of adventures while doing it. Hansje remembered the author's name, Anne de Vries because it was the same as his Aunt Anne who lived in Friesland. Every day, when the teacher read another chapter to the class, everyone sat very still and listened very carefully. Especially Hansje.

One day, two men came to the school and spent some time in each classroom. When they came into the grade four classroom, the teacher stopped the lesson and introduced the men.

"These men are inspectors for our Christian schools," the teacher said. "They come every year to find out how well you are learning. They are going to ask you some questions, so when you know the answer, put up your hand, and you can give the answer."

The first questions were easy.

"Who was the baby who was put in a basket in the reeds by the Nile river?" All the hands went up. The answer was "Moses," of course.

The next question was easy, too, "Who was the strongest man who ever lived?"

Everyone knew the answer, "Samson."

But then one inspector asked,

"What was the name of the girl who picked up stalks of grain that the reapers had missed?" The only hand up was Hansje's.

"Yes, do you know the answer?"

"Yes, it was Gerdientje!" Hansje said loudly, happy to see that he was the only one who knew the answer.

But the inspector didn't nod and say, "Very good." Instead, he looked confused, especially when the whole class burst out laughing. The teacher frowned. Hansje was confused, too. Hadn't the teacher just read that chapter about Jaap and Gerdientje reaping and gleaning to the class yesterday?

Then the inspector explained, "The answer is Ruth."

Yes, of course, Hansje knew that story, too. Ruth gleaned in the field of Boaz, and later they married each other. Mama had read the story many times from the Children's Bible, and he always looked at the picture of Ruth bending over, picking up grain.

Hansje looked down, his face getting hot and red. Why hadn't he thought of Ruth instead of Gerdientje? Now it was too late. Now everyone thought he was a dummy. And he hated that.

But wait a minute! No one else had said, "Ruth," or even "Gerdientje." But he had because he loved stories and remembered them better than anyone else in the class. That made him feel a little better.

22 Hansje Plays a Serious Game of Tag

Hansje, the boy who loved to go fast, had a big problem. His feet and ankles always started to hurt after he walked or ran for a long time. By late afternoon, his feet hurt even when he was just standing still.

When he told Papa and Mama, they took him to a foot doctor, the same one that Papa always went to. After the doctor had checked his feet, he said, "Hansje, you have a foot problem just like your Papa. You have fallen arches, which people call flat feet, and you need to wear high top shoes with some special metal soles inside your shoes to help support your feet."

Hansje smiled because usually going to a doctor meant getting pricked with a needle which he didn't like at all. But he knew getting fitted for foot supports wouldn't hurt.

So, a week later the strong, hard metal foot supports were ready and Papa put them into Hansje's new high top shoes. When Hansje stood up and walked around, Papa asked, "So, how do they feel?"

"Sort of heavy and clunky, and I can't bend my feet very well in these high-top shoes," Hansje said.

"You'll get used to them," Papa said, "I got used to mine too."

Hansje still complained sometimes because his shoes were rather clunky. But even though they were not as good as the soft but firm kind of arch supports as we have now, the metal ones worked fine. Now Hansje could stand, walk, and run all day long without his feet hurting.

Hansje needed to run fast at school because he and his friends were always playing tag, and, of course, if he didn't run fast, he would always be *IT*, which is no fun.

The kind of tag Hansje and his friends played was quite different from the ordinary tag kids play these days. Hansje and his friends played a very serious game of tag. They didn't just play it for a few minutes at recess or at lunch time and then quit like kids do now. Oh, no! They played one long game of tag, all day long, and into the next day, and the next week, through the whole school year.

Yes, this was the game that never ends.
It just goes on and on my friends.
Some kids just started playing it,
not knowing what it was,
and they continued playing it forever just
because,
this was the game that never ends.

One day, Hansje's friend Wim tagged him just as he was leaving the schoolyard and Hansje wasn't allowed to tag him back. He looked around to see if there was anyone else in the game still walking around, but there was no one. So, he had to walk home being *IT*.

He thought about how much he hated being *IT* as he walked home. He thought about being *IT* when he was doing his homework and when he was having supper. He thought about being *IT* when he lay in bed at night. He even thought about praying to God about being *IT* but didn't think that was serious enough for God, so he didn't. The next morning, as soon as he got up, he thought about being *IT* again and still didn't like it.

When he got to school, as soon as he saw Piet, one of his tag game friends, he casually walked up to him and tagged him and whispered. "Tag, you're *IT*." Piet looked confused. "Hey, I thought Wim was *IT* last night, and he isn't at school yet!"

"Yes, but Wim tagged me at the end of school," Hansje said.

Right away Piet started walking casually up to

their friend Jan who was just arriving at school. "Tag, you're *IT*!" Piet said, and the game was on its way again.

Hansje was very careful all day long, keeping track of who was *IT*, and staying away from him. Finally, it was late in the afternoon, soon the bell would ring, and his class would file out of the classroom, walk down the hall and out the front door.

Hansje knew that his friend Geert [GIT] was *IT* and would probably be standing right outside the door, waiting for him to come out so he could tag him. Then Hansje would be *IT* again. He hated the idea so much he started thinking of some way out of it.

Suddenly he had the best idea of the day. The classroom had two doors, the front one everyone was supposed to use and one at the back, which was for emergencies only. *Well,* Hansje thought, *this is sort of an emergency.*

No sooner did he think of it than the bell rang. He stood up with all the rest of the students but didn't walk with them to the door. Instead, he walked to the back of the classroom and pretended to look at the books on the bookshelf by the back door.

He waited until the teacher turned around to clean something off the blackboard and Zip! Hansje was out the door and scooting down the hallway. No one was supposed to be in that hallway, so as soon as he got to the school side door, he flung it open, ran out into the alley, and WHACK! BAM!!

The next thing Hansje knew was that he was lying on his back alongside a big black taxi that had been driving slowly down the alley along the school.

Hansje lay there with one leg sort of under the taxi, looking very surprised. Kids were running up to look, and the taxi driver jumped out shouting, "He just ran out of that door right in front of me, and I couldn't stop!"

He knelt by Hansje and then both he and Hansje noticed that the right front wheel had run right over Hansje's foot. It looked horrible. The leather of his new high top shoes was all cut up, and the foot looked smashed. Who knows how many bones were broken?

In no time, lots of kids crowded all around, and a couple of teachers arrived wearing concerned looks. Suddenly Hansje felt a hand touch him on the shoulder as he lay there. "Tag, you're *IT*," Geert whispered.

Yes, they played a very serious game of tag in that school.

Then the principal pushed his way through the crowd. "What's going on here?' he asked sternly.

"This boy suddenly came running out of the side door and ran right in front of my taxi," the driver explained. "I had no time to stop."

The teachers were now on their knees beside Hansje and very carefully took off his shoe and sock. They tenderly poked his foot and asked if it hurt.

"No," Hansje replied, "It doesn't hurt at all." The teachers looked at each other in surprise and kept poking and twisting his foot, but nothing hurt.

One teacher helped him to stand up, while the other examined Hansje's shoe. It was all cut up from the inside. He showed it to the other teacher. They couldn't figure it out until suddenly he pulled out the metal insole. It was bent and twisted, and the edge of the insole had cut the leather of the shoe on both sides. But it had protected Hansje's foot. Not a single bone was broken. He didn't even have a scratch or a bruise. Everyone was relieved that he wasn't hurt.

But when Hansje stood up and saw his cut up and ruined shoe, he began to sob and cry.

"Why are you crying?" the principal asked, "Does your foot hurt when you stand on it?"

Hansje just shook his head and kept sniffing. "Well then, why are you crying?" the principal asked again.

"Because I'm going to get a spanking for wrecking my new shoe when I get home," Hansje said and sobbed even louder.

The principal, however, was so happy that it was only Hansje's shoe that was wrecked, and not his foot that he promised to phone Hansje's Papa right away.

"I'll explain that it was a car accident with a taxi and that you could have been badly hurt but weren't." That would help; maybe Hansje wouldn't get a spanking after all.

He walked home, with his metal insole in his hand, hobbling a bit since his shoe was all cut, loose and floppy.

On the way home, he suddenly remembered that Geert had tagged him as he lay with his leg under the taxi. He hated being *IT*, but this time he hated something else even worse, walking home with a wrecked shoe.

When he got home, Mama hugged him, and Papa checked out the wrecked shoe and the bent insole. Then they told him the principal had phoned them and told them it was mostly the taxi's fault for driving so close to the school door. Papa didn't reach for the carpet beater, so Hansje was very happy, and after he said his regular bedtime prayer, he even told God how happy he was.

The next day the shoemaker fixed up the shoe, stitching some extra leather over the cuts, and the doctor hammered the insole back into shape. Hansje never complained again about having to wear metal insoles.

Meanwhile, back at school, it was the game of tag that never ends, it just goes on and on my friends . . . .

23 Hansje Throws More Stones

Even when Hansje was very young, he liked to throw stones. And when he was eight years old, he still liked throwing stones, but he wasn't very good at it. He could throw fast, but he couldn't throw straight so he hardly ever hit what he aimed for. While walking to school he'd sometimes see some stray dogs across the street and throw a stone at them, but the dogs would just look at him, shrug their shoulders, and walk away slowly because they were safe.

He never hit anything, except one time, and that time he hit something he wished he hadn't hit.

Now everyone knows that mamas know what their kids like to do. Hansje's Mama knew that her little son loved to throw stones. That's why every day when he got ready to walk to school, she would say, "Remember what I told you. Don't throw stones." Sometimes she would even shake her finger and frown at him.

Hansje would nod, as all kids do when their moms tell them not to do things. But by the time he got to the first driveway, the one with lots of nice throwing stones lying in it, he would already have forgotten what Mama had said. He would pick up a couple of stones and start flinging them into the branches of trees, and at boards in fences, or garbage cans or whatever looked like a good target.

One day Hansje was playing with Arnold, one of his friends. He lived right across the street from Hansje in a nice, big house with large front windows. His dad owned a lumberyard, and Arnold's family was quite rich. Arnold was a little younger and a bit smaller than Hansje, but he acted big, probably because he lived in a big house. He liked pestering Hansje just like little brothers and sisters sometimes like to pester their older brothers or sisters.

Sometimes Hansje and Arnold would be playing nicely together on the driveway in front of Arnold's house when suddenly Arnold would start screaming and crying. Naturally, Arnold's Mama would rush out of their house, and Arnold would point his finger at Hansje and cry, "Hansje hurt me! Hansje hurt me!"

Sometimes it wasn't even true. He just did it to get

attention. But most of the time he would play nice for a long time.

One day, Arnold and Hansje had been playing happily together, when suddenly Arnold grabbed a stick that Hansje had found and stepped in the middle of it while pulling up on one end.

So, naturally, the stick broke. That was bad enough, but then he started whacking Hansje with it. So, Hansje stooped down and grabbed a handful of small stones and threw them at Arnold.

The stones didn't hurt him because they were very small like peas and Hansje didn't throw very hard because Arnold was standing right in front of him trying to hit him some more with the piece of stick.

But then Arnold ran towards his house laughing, and Hansje picked up another handful of peas gravel stones and threw them as hard has he could at Arnold who was running away and looking over his shoulder laughing at Hansje.

The hail of peas gravel hit him a little harder than before, but not hard enough to hurt. But, "Uh oh," among the pea sized stones there was also a stone the size of a very large marble.

It went flying towards Arnold too. But it didn't hit him. Oh no. It flew right past him and hit Arnold's house. No, that's not quite right. It hit the big front window in Arnold's house. And where it hit, it made a small hole with some big white splinters sticking out in all directions like a star.

Well, when Arnold saw the hole in the window, he started to yell as loudly as he could, "Papa! Mama!

Hansje broke our window! Hansje threw a stone and broke our window!"

It was true, even though the window wasn't in small pieces, it did have a small hole in it, and the cracks would probably spread across the whole window.

Arnold's Mama came running out of her house. Arnold's dad came running out of the office at the back. Hansje's Mama came running out of her house across the street still carrying her dust cloth. And last of all, Hansje's Papa left his fish shop behind the house and still wearing his messy fish butcher apron, walked quickly across the street, taking large steps as he always did when he was angry.

That's when Hansje started wishing he had obeyed Mama when she warned him not to throw stones.

The two fathers walked to the window and stood there poking at the hole with their fingers. Then they turned around and looked at Hansje. The two mothers were looking at Hansje and, of course, Arnold was looking at Hansje, too, but he was also sticking his tongue out at him when nobody could see him do it.

Everybody knew what was coming next. Papa took Hansje by the arm and with Hansje running along beside him, walked quickly to the back of the house. There he grabbed the big carpet beater that always hung from a nail on the wall near the back door. He turned Hansje over his knee and spanked him with the carpet beater. He never said a word the whole time he was spanking Hansje, but Hansje made up for it by crying and screaming very loud and very long, even longer than the spanking lasted.

Then they went into the house, and Mama said, "Didn't I tell you not to throw stones? Now, look what happened. Windows that big cost a lot of money and now we have to pay to put in a new one."

Hansje had to go to bed without supper and lay there thinking for a while before he went to sleep.

Maybe my Mama and Papa are right. Maybe they just knew something bad might happen when kids throw stones. Maybe they know more than I do.

He even thought about praying about this stones throwing problem. But then he thought, *Maybe God is just as angry with me as my Papa and Mama,* so he didn't say anything and finally went to sleep.

Did Hansje ever throw any more stones? Well, maybe he was a little more careful near windows, but . . . stop totally?

Probably not.

24 Hansje Eats a White Bird

Hansje did not like to eat fish. And no wonder. He was surrounded by every kind of fish, large and small, scaly and slimy, alive and dead. He saw them every day. He smelled them every day, and he touched them so much that his hands and clothes always seemed to smell of fish.

No, he didn't live at the bottom of the sea. But he might as well have since Papa had a store in which he sold fish for people to eat. Not only did Papa buy fish from the fishermen, but before he sold them, he had to clean the guts out of the fish. That way the customers wouldn't have those nasty fish guts to smell up their garbage. And guess who helped Papa when the store was busy, and lots of fish had to be cleaned? Yes, of course, it was Hansje, his oldest son.

Since he was only nine years old, he couldn't reach the fish cleaning workbench, so he had to stand on a wooden box. On the workbench stood a large, shallow bin full of fish, sometimes fifty herring in it, sometimes five or six codfish or a dozen mackerel.

Hansje knew what to do. He grabbed a fish, and if they had scales, he scraped the scales off, then cut the belly open, scraped the guts out, cut off the fins and the head, rinsed the fish in clean water and laid it neatly on a tray. Then he took the next one. He scraped, cut, rinsed and stacked fish, over and over again, for as long as it took to empty the bin.

He always struggled to gut the snakelike eels that kept wriggling and wrapping themselves around his forearm as he cut their long bellies open. Even after he scraped out all their guts and cut off their heads, they would keep twisting. He cut up big, flat stingrays being careful not to touch their stingers. He whacked big codfish on their heads with a wooden mallet, just in case they were still alive before he started cutting them up.

Hansje had learned about those sneaky codfish several years before when he was still a very small boy. He had seen a dead codfish lying on the counter with its mouth open. He looked into its mouth and saw the rows of teeth. So, he reached his hand into the codfish's mouth to feel how sharp the teeth were. They were very sharp, as he found out when the codfish proved he was still alive and snapped his huge jaws closed on Hansje's hand.

He yelled until Papa came to pry open the jaws and take his little hand out, all full of blood. Hansje had never seen that much of his own blood before and for a few moments, he thought he was going to die and thought about God. But he didn't die. He did, however, learn to whack the codfish on the head with a large wooden mallet before cutting them open and cleaning the guts out of them.

He worked with cold and dead fish, with cold and wriggling fish, with salted herring and smoked eels, and he even fried fish in the two deep, square frying pans at the back of the store. They were smoking hot, and Papa was always very serious when he showed Hansje how to fry the fish in that boiling oil.

The kids at school sometimes wrinkled their noses at his fishy smell, and pointed at him, especially when he forgot to clean the fish scales off his shoes.

No wonder when he sat down to eat lunch he would much rather eat a piece of chicken, or beef or pork. Anything that didn't look or smell like fish, or had fish bones in it.

Oh, yes, that was the other thing. Ever since he was very small, Mama had been warning him, "Be careful of the fish bones! Don't choke on the fish bones!"

So naturally, Hansje was afraid of choking on fish bones every time he took even a small bite of fish. He especially didn't like the yucky, slimy white sauce that Mama always poured over his piece of fish.

Of course, Hansje wasn't always working when he was with Papa. Sometimes he went for a car ride with Papa to the harbour when Papa bought fish from the fishermen. He loved seeing the ships and the beach, although he didn't appreciate seeing and smelling the hundreds of wooden crates, with thousands of fish, that the fishermen brought ashore for Papa to poke at and look over to see which ones he wanted to buy.

One day Hansje walked away from all those crates of fish and looked up into the sky. He loved watching the big white birds, so white, bright, and beautiful as they soared high in the blue sky, swooping down to the salty waves and back up again. When Papa called him to come and have lunch, he was still thinking of those white birds.

While they were waiting for the sandwich man to bring them something to eat, Hansje said to Papa, "You know those big white birds? I bet they would be good to eat. Their meat would be so white and would taste even better than chicken."

"Oh yes," Papa said, "those white birds are very good to eat. Maybe someday we'll have one for lunch."

Sure enough, a week or so later Hansje sat down with Mama, Papa, his cute little sister Jannie, and his little brother Wobbie. Then Mama put some white meat on his plate. "That is some white bird meat," Papa said.

Wow! Hansje ate it all up and then asked for more. Yes, he liked to eat white bird meat, it was much more tender than chicken. He didn't have to worry about choking on sharp little fish bones, and it didn't have any yucky slimy white sauce on it. He was glad they often had it. But then, one day, something very strange happened.

He was taking the guts out of a big codfish when Papa gave him a piece of newspaper and told him to cut the codfish in half and wrap the big half in the newspaper. When he was wrapping it up, he saw a picture of a very fat man in the newspaper and laughed to himself about how very fat that man was.

When he finished with the codfish, he went on to the job that he liked the most. He took the water hose and squirted water at the hundreds of big, black flies buzzing up and down the huge windows above the rinse tanks. He loved to spray the water and wash all those flies down into the tank and down the drain hole. Papa liked him to do that too. He didn't want flies crawling all over the trays of nice cleaned fish. Customers didn't like to see the fish they were going to buy with flies crawling on it, either.

All that water splashing and fly drowning, made Hansje feel like he had to go pee, so he went into the house to the bathroom. When he was finished, Mama called from the kitchen, "Hansje, will you take the kitchen garbage out and throw it into the outside bin?"

"Okay," he said, and picked up the pail of kitchen garbage. As he dumped it in the outside bin, he saw a piece of wet newspaper on the top, and he could clearly see the picture of a very fat man.

Wait a minute! That was the same newspaper he had wrapped the piece of codfish in earlier. So, they were going to have codfish for lunch. Well, he wasn't going to eat any.

At lunch time when Hansje sat down with everyone else, Mama smiled as she put a piece of white meat on his plate and said, "Here is some more white bird meat that you like so much."

Hansje looked around the table and saw a piece of white meat on everyone's plate. Then he noticed that Papa and Mama poured yucky, white sauce all over their white meat. Suddenly he realized what had been going on.

Mama had been giving him codfish to eat and telling him it was white meat from a white bird. But all the time he had been eating fish without yucky, slimy, white sauce on it, thinking it was white bird meat. And he had liked it!

What a dirty trick Papa and Mama had played on him! Just to show them they couldn't trick him anymore, he refused to eat his fish, no matter how much Papa and Mama told him it was white bird meat.

And he kept on eating as little fish as he possibly could. Right up until the time he grew up and moved to Canada. Then he started catching fish in the river and ate lots of them.

But not with that yucky, slimy, white sauce on it. No way!

25 Hansje Takes a Short Cut

Hansje loved to go fast all his life. Mama always warned him not to run fast, or skate fast, or bike fast. But Hansje didn't listen. Of course, not. He was a boy who loved to go fast much more than he loved to obey Mama. Yes, he was. But one day something happened that made him wish he had listened to Mama when she said, "Don't bike too fast."

Even though Hansje liked to go fast, he was not a bad boy. He always went to Sunday school on Sunday mornings when he was little and, after his tenth birthday, he also wanted to go to the special Sunday evening youth church for kids ten years old and older.

He told Mama and Papa that he wanted to go to the special church for kids and young people on Sunday evening and Mama said, "Okay, I'll go with you."

So, the next Sunday Hansje and Mama got on their bicycles and biked to the special service. Hansje really liked it, so he went every Sunday night, and Mama always went with him because she didn't like him to ride his bike home after dark. They always went on their bikes because in his country everybody rode bikes wherever they had to go, and they hardly ever used cars.

But one Sunday evening as they were biking back from the church Hansje said, "Mama, let's go down this other street for a change. It's a short cut."

Mama didn't want to go that way, but she said, "Well, if you want to go that way, you go ahead, but I am going straight home, I'm tired and want to sit down with your Papa and rest for a while before going to bed. You go ahead, but, remember, don't bike too fast."

Hansje said, "Okay, I'll go this way, and I bet I'll beat you home." He was quite happy that Mama wasn't with him because she always biked so slow that it was very boring. Now that he was going alone on the short cut, he could bike as fast as he wanted even though Mama had said, "Don't bike too fast."

Hansje turned the corner to the shortcut and started peddling as hard as he could. Soon he could see a little hill and couldn't wait to go down it so he could go even faster. Down he went, peddling very hard on his bike, going very fast, right down the middle of the road since there were no cars on the street at all.

The wind was whistling past his ears; his eyes were watering from the wind because he was going so fast, and he couldn't see very well. Too bad he couldn't see, because up ahead there was something that was going to cause him a lot of trouble.

Everyone knows that most streets have big, round manhole covers right in the middle of the street. Sometimes a worker has to go down those holes to fix things underneath the street, like water pipes. Well, what Hansje didn't know was that about halfway down the hill one of those manholes covers was on crooked and was sticking up a little.

It is no surprise that Hansje, going faster on his bike than he had ever gone in his life, ran into that crooked manhole cover with his bike. Naturally, his bike's front wheel twisted a little, and because the bike was going so fast, it flipped over, and Hansje went flying through the air and landed on the road, banging his head, and then slid and rolled into a tree at the side of the road. There he lay, while his bike rolled on and banged into another tree and just lay there. And then it was very quiet. Hansje wasn't crying or anything; he was just lying there very quiet, all limp like he was sleeping.

But he wasn't sleeping, oh no. He was dizzy and couldn't see very well, and everything seemed to be moving around him. Then some people came running out of a nearby house, picked him up, and carried him inside. They put cold, wet towels on his head and gave him some water to drink. Then they asked him, "What is your name? What is the phone number of your Mama's and Papa's house?"

So he told them, "My name is Hansje, and our phone number is 7181." It was a very short phone number since they didn't have very many phones in those days. The people phoned Mama and Papa and told them their boy had fallen off his bike, and that it looked like he would be okay, but he would be home a little later.

After a while, Hansje got up and got back on his bike that the people had found further down the hill and brought back to the house. Then he pedaled home very slowly and carefully. As he pedaled, his head started to hurt. By the time he got home, it was very dark; and he was very pale, felt very sick, and he threw up when he got inside, so Mama and Papa called the doctor, and he came over to have a look.

After he looked in Hansje's eyes and checked the bumps on his head, he said, "He has had a bad bang on his head and has shaken up his brain very badly. This is called a brain concussion. He needs to lie flat on his back in a dark, quiet room for three days, with his eyes closed. Nobody is allowed to talk to him. He can eat but only a little bit, and he can't sit up to eat, he has to keep lying flat on his back. After three days, I'll come back and look at him again."

And that is what happened. Hansje lay on his back with his eyes closed in a dark room for three whole days and three whole nights. At first, he slept a lot, but he didn't know if it was night or day since the room was dark all the time. He was not very happy, not even after the first day when his head stopped hurting. He never heard any voices or music or even any house noises, except when Mama whispered to him when she came to feed him or when he had to go to the bathroom.

He couldn't read or listen to the radio. He could do nothing at all but lie in a dark room for three whole days and nights. He had lots of time to think, to sleep, and to think about God. Sometimes he even prayed to God, even though he felt guilty about riding his bike so fast down that hill when Mama had told him not to.

At the end, when the doctor came back and said, "Okay, you can get up now," he felt as if he had been lying there for weeks.

His parents hoped that from then on their son would never again want to ride his bike fast. But he did. I guess it takes more than a three-day concussion to stop a boy like Hansje from wanting to go fast.

26 Hansje Cuts His Hand

One morning when Hansje was nine years old, and in a hurry to get to school, a very bad thing happened to him.

It all started at breakfast which was late because Papa and Mama were so busy listening to the radio. He hurriedly ate his porridge, and as he gulped his milk, they told him what they had heard on the radio.

"Princess Juliana and Prince Bernhard have just had their fourth baby," Papa said. And Mama added, "She is called Christiana."

When Hansje heard that, he was even more in a hurry, and nearly spilled the last bit of his milk. He knew there would be a big party at school to celebrate the birth of the new royal baby. And he really didn't want to miss the special goodies everyone always ate to celebrate the birth of a baby. With a royal baby, it would be even more special.

Since it was the middle of February when it's always cold and wet, he put on his winter jacket and dashed out the door. He ran half a block, then walked half a block, then ran again.

He hated getting to school late. It had happened once the previous year when he was in grade two. When he got to school, the door was locked. He had to ring the bell. The janitor came to let him in and took him to his classroom. Then, instead of going out to play at recess, he had to stay in to explain why he was late. He didn't want that to happen again.

Hansje was only three blocks from school when he took his usual shortcut through a muddy alley behind a hotel. Halfway through the alley he started to run again and suddenly slipped on some icy mud and fell on his hands and knees. When he got up, the heel of his left hand hurt a lot and was bleeding heavily. He pulled his hanky out of his pocket and wadded it up against the cut to slow down the bleeding, then he turned around and sadly walked home.

As he walked, he tried to ask God to let his hand not hurt so much, but he also was sort of unhappy with God. "Why did you let me fall?" he wanted to ask. But he didn't because he had been running in a muddy alley which he knew, even without Mama telling him, that he shouldn't have been doing. He felt it was his own fault, so he didn't dare to ask God to make things better.

"Why did you come back?" Mama asked and quickly added, "Why are you so muddy? Did you fall? Didn't I tell you not to run and fall? Why don't you . . . .?"

Hansje didn't say anything; he just held up his left hand with the bloody handkerchief in it from which blood dripped onto the hall floor. That stopped the questions, as Mama ran out the back door to get Papa. He ran into the house, carefully lifted the handkerchief and looked at the cut with blood still coming out of it.

"Let's go," he said, and they got into their little delivery van and drove straight to the house of the family doctor. Dr. Esselink took Hansje into his front room which was painted all white and smelled of bleach. He carefully washed out the cut with peroxide which foamed all over his hand but didn't sting.

"No iodine," Hansje said in a quivery voice, "please don't put on iodine." He hated it when he had a little cut or scrape, and Mama would get out the first aid kit and put drops of iodine on the cut to kill the germs. Hansje was sure it would kill germs since it stung and burned so much.

"Don't worry," the doctor said, "it's a nice clean wound. It bled a lot, so I'll just clean the skin around it some more, and then we'll close it up and bandage it."

He did all that, but it seemed to take a long time and hurt quite a bit, especially when he stapled the wound shut with a medical instrument that looked like a pair of pliers. He wouldn't let Hansje look at what he was doing until his hand was all nicely bandaged, and it wasn't hurting anymore.

While Hansje had his left hand stretched out and looking in the other direction, the way the doctor had told him to, he wondered if God knew about his cut. He figured God did, but he asked God anyway, "Please don't let it hurt anymore and make it all better soon."

On the way home, Hansje said, "I want to go to school." Papa was so surprised; he nearly swerved into a man riding a bicycle. "What, you don't want to go home and rest?"

"No, I want to go to school. They'll be celebrating the birth of the new princess, and I want to eat the goodies and drink lemonade." Papa laughed and said, "Okay, I understand. I'll drop you off at school."

So Hansje arrived very late, rang the bell, and the janitor took him to his classroom. When he showed his bandaged hand to the teacher and told him that he fell and cut himself, there was no problem. He was also very happy to see that the eating part of the celebration hadn't started yet. They had already sung the national anthem, and the teacher had written on the blackboard:

"Welcome to her royal highness, Princess Cristiana!"

Hansje put up his hand, not the one with the bandage on it which he kept quietly lying in his lap. "Yes, Hansje," the teacher said, "Do you have a question?"

"Instead of 'her royal *high*ness; shouldn't it be . . .' her royal *small*ness'?" That made all the kids in his grade three class laugh. But the teacher just frowned at him and said, "No!"

Late in the morning, the baker arrived and the celebration began. Everyone got a glass of lemonade at their desk. Then the baker came around and gave everyone a *beschuit met muisjes.* Those words mean "rusk with little mice." A rusk is a thick, round, piece of very dry toast, but tastes a lot better than ordinary toast. Then they spread butter on the rusk and sprinkle on a thick layer of the "little mice" which are actually tiny coloured sugar balls that are flavoured with aniseed. For a boy baby, the sugar sprinkles are always coloured white and blue. For a girl baby, they are white and pink. But these were white and orange because orange is the royal colour in Holland. It was because of the rusks with the sugar sprinkles that Hansje wanted to make sure he was at school on that Tuesday, February 18, in 1947. He ate as many as the baker gave him.

At noon, all the kids in his class crowded around him to look at his bandaged hand and asked him what happened. As he started to tell how he was running and slipped and fell, he knew they would ask him what he had cut his hand on. He would have to say, "I don't know, something sharp. Maybe a broken bottle or a sharp piece of gravel?"

But that sounded so ordinary it would be boring. So he invented a better ending. "It was some very sharp metal, probably a piece of a hand-grenade left over from the war."

Days later, as he told the story again and again to other kids, he improved on it and just said, "I fell on a sharp piece of a hand grenade." That made it sound like it was a war wound. He liked that ending much better.

Later, the doctor unwrapped the bandages, and with another instrument that looked like a small, shiny pair of pliers, he took out the staples. It hurt when he did that, but Hansje forgot about it when he saw he had a big scar. He measured it with his ruler when he got home and was happy to see it was about three centimetres long. It never went away. No other boy had that kind of scar.

Later, he improved the story even more. Sometimes he told how during the war a grenade exploded and he was wounded in the hand as he held it up in front of his face. Or sometimes it was to shield a friend. At other times, he would tell it as if he ran from enemy soldiers who were shooting and tripped and fell onto a sharp shard of grenade or piece of shrapnel from a bomb.

Yes, even when Hansje was only nine years old, he already liked making stories more interesting. Later, when Hansje was a daddy, and even later when he was a grandpa, he explained his scar a little more truthfully, "I was running to make sure I got in on the school celebration of the newly born princess, and I fell. I landed on something sharp, probably a piece of broken beer bottle, but, it *could* have been a piece of a grenade or maybe even a piece of a bomb."

27 Hansje is Curious About a Flower Display

One day towards the end of March, when Hansje was nine years old, he was riding in the van with Papa when they stopped in front of a flower shop. Papa got out and said, "I'm going to buy some flowers for Mama's birthday. You stay here in the van. I'll be back in a minute." He crossed the sidewalk and walked into the flower shop to pick out some flowers.

Hansje rolled down his window and peered at the flower shop window. He couldn't see Papa, but he saw all sorts of colors, probably from displays of flowers. There seemed to be a lot right close to the window.

Hansje liked flowers. He wondered what kinds of flowers were in the shop. So many flowers would smell nice, and he wished he could smell them. He wondered what kind of flowers Papa was going to buy for Mama. He looked and looked; he even sniffed, but he couldn't see many flowers, and he sure couldn't smell any. Then he had an idea.

It was a good idea, he opened the van door, crossed the sidewalk, very quietly opened the door of the flower shop, and sneaked inside. As quietly as possible he closed the door behind him. He could see Papa talking with the flower shop owner who was showing him different kinds of flowers. *I'll hide here behind the flower stand,* Hansje thought, *and very quietly watch until Papa finishes choosing the flowers. Then, when he is paying for them as the florist wraps them up, I'll quietly open the door, slip out and be back sitting in the van when Papa comes out.*

He thought it was a great idea, so he stood next to the door right by a tall display with lots of flowers in vases next to the window. He loved the flowers and the smells all around him. It was so much better than sitting in the van and being bored.

He leaned against that tall flower case so he could smell some yellow flowers just above his nose. He leaned just a little, not pushing it or anything like that, but suddenly the whole display case started to fall!

Shelves crashed, broken glass tinkled, and boards slipped and tipped. Pots fell to the ground and spilled dirt and plants out onto the floor. Worst of all, a dozen vases fell and broke, splashing water and dumping flowers everywhere. The store owner ran towards the mess, his mouth and eyes wide open. Papa ran right behind him, shouting, "Didn't I tell you to stay in the van? Go and sit in it, now!"

Hansje ran out of the store and sat in the van feeling very scared. Papa was very angry, and he would surely get a spanking when he got home.

After a long time, Papa came out of the store carrying a bunch of yellow flowers. He put them in the back, got into the front, and as they drove home, he scolded Hansje for a long time. "You are so disobedient! You should have stayed in the van as I told you! You broke all those vases and wrecked so many plants and flowers. I had to pay a lot of money to the store owner."

By the time they got home, he had calmed down a bit. He gave the flowers to Hansje's Mama and wished her a Happy Birthday. As she was getting a vase to put them in, Papa grabbed Hansje's hand and started walking to the back door where the carpet beater hung. Hansje started to cry because he knew he was going to get a spanking.

"What's happening?" Mama asked. So Papa told her about Hansje being disobedient, leaning against the flower display, breaking all those vases with flowers, and about how he had to pay a lot of money.

Mama looked at Hansje and shook her head. "You are just too curious," she said. Then she turned to Papa and said, "Don't spank him. His crying would spoil my happy birthday."

Hansje was very happy when he heard that. He stopped sniffling when Papa let go of his hand, and he smiled brightly and hugged Mama and said, "Happy birthday, Mama! I'll never be curious again." I'm sure he meant it. But it's impossible to stop a boy like Hansje from being curious and wanting to find out things for himself.

That night, after he said his usual prayer, he whispered, "Thank you for my Mama and Papa. And Jesus, please help me to obey them even when I'm curious and want to do things they don't want me to do. Oh, and thank you that I didn't get a spanking."

28 Hansje Skates Too Far and Too Fast

When Hansje was nine years old, he was often afraid he would do something that would make him die. I guess it was because Hansje's Mama was afraid her boy might get sick, or get in an accident, or get lost, or get hurt badly, or die, so she always told him, "Be careful! Don't run too fast! You might run in front of a car, get run over and die. Don't ride your bike too fast! You might run into a tree and die. Don't get your feet wet; you might get pneumonia and die. Don't ever get too wet or too cold in the snow because you might get a fever and cough, feel terribly sick, and die."

She was especially afraid of pneumonia because one of Hansje's uncles had been wet and cold, got sick with a fever and lots of coughing, and died. So Hansje, even though he was young, was afraid to die. But he still wanted to run fast and bike fast. Yes, Hansje was a boy who loved to go fast.

One cold winter day Hansje got up from eating his breakfast and walked to school as he did every day. Well, not quite every day, not on Sundays, because there was no school on Sundays. But this was a

Saturday, and he went off to school, but just for the morning, because on Wednesdays and Saturdays, he went to school only in the mornings.

This particular Saturday morning Hansje walked to school in on icy streets with all the puddles frozen hard. There was even some snow. When he got to school, he joined his friends and heard them talking about how they were going to go skating on the lake in the afternoon.

Hey, great idea! Hansje loved to go skating because with skates you can go a lot faster than just running. So, he could hardly wait for the morning to end so he could run home, eat his lunch, and ask Mama if he could go skating on the lake. Mama said, "Sure, you can go skating. There are lots of people skating there today. But take a scarf and make sure you don't get too cold because then you will get pneumonia and die."

All winter long she had been reminding him not to get cold and wet because he would get pneumonia and die.

And, of course, she also told him, "Don't skate too fast and look carefully where you are going, or you might run into somebody, fall down, and hurt yourself."

That is what Hansje's Mama said, but all he heard was, "Sure, you can go skating." He never listened to anything Mama said about not going too fast. But this time, he should have listened.

He ran upstairs, grabbed his long yellow skates with the brown leather straps, and ran back down the stairs. He put on his thick wool sweater, his warm jacket, his wool mittens, his warm woolen cap, and his scarf, and ran out the door. The lake was quite a long way away, but he was happy to walk for a half an hour to get there. He was a good walker because he walked to school every day, so his legs were good and strong. Also, he ran a lot because he was a boy who liked to go fast.

When he got to the lake, he sat down on a stump and tied his skates to the bottom of his shoes. He tied them very tightly and made sure they were pointed straight ahead. Everyone had the kind of skates he had, the kind you tie on. Nobody had skates like today that have their own shoes fastened right on them.

When his skates were on tight, he stepped onto the lake and started skating. It was perfect. The ice was smooth, hard, and black. The wind had blown all the snow off the lake and had polished the ice so it couldn't be better for skating. And yes, there were many other people skating, too. Lots of men were going very fast, and he tried to keep up with them. Then he played tag with a bunch of boys from the neighbourhood and school, and that was lots of fun. But, he noticed the wind was blowing hard and when he was skating into the wind, he couldn't go very fast.

So, he thought, *if going against the wind slows me down, then going with the wind would speed me up.* He was right of course. The moment he figured that out, he had a plan. He skated to the north end of the lake, against the wind and then turned around to skate south with the north wind pushing him on his back.

He skated hard, the north wind blowing him along. He skated very fast and nearly ran into some adults as they were skating around in a large circle. But he skated right past them without hitting anyone and as he did, he thought, *Those silly people, why are they going around in a circle at one end of the lake when you can go in a straight line, all the way to the other end of the lake?* He was about to find out.

When you skate on a skating rink, there is concrete or dirt, but under the ice of a lake, there is water. When people start skating on a lake, the ice is usually thick and strong and will hold up lots of people skating on it. But sometimes on other parts of the lake, the ice might be quite thin and will hold only one person. And in other parts of the lake the ice is so thin, it won't hold even one person, not even if that person is a nine-year-old boy on skates going very fast. Sometimes there were even places where there was no ice at all, just water.

But Hansje didn't know much about lakes, and he didn't care. He was the boy who loved to go fast, and he was going very fast and loving it. The wind blew at his back and pushed him along. The bright sun shone on his face, and he squinted his eyes so they wouldn't water so much. That's probably why he didn't see that the glare on the ice ahead of him was not the sun shining on ice, but the sun shining on water! Yes, he was skating straight for the open water. Suddenly he saw the shining black water rippling in the wind right ahead of him. He tried to stop or turn, but before the thought could travel down to his feet, he splashed into the icy water and went all the way under.

What a shock! It was cold and wet and dark down there. Then it got even colder! Of course, he could swim very well, but that was in the summer wearing a swimsuit. But now it was winter, and he was wearing his heavy winter jacket, his wool cap, his wool sweater, his wool mittens, and his scarf. They were wet and heavy, heavy, heavy, dragging him down. Also, his long, pointed skates kept getting tangled in weeds growing up from the bottom of the lake.

But he held his breath and kept kicking and swimming up, even though his wet clothes kept dragging him down. Finally, he got his head out of the water, took a deep breath, and swam to the edge of the ice. He tried to grab it, but it broke off because it was so thin. Then he splashed and struggled some more and broke some more ice off.

While he was doing this, he was afraid and thought he might die. Then he thought about God, even though it was not meal time or bed time, and in his thoughts, he asked God to not let him drown or freeze to death.

Then he saw some men racing towards him. One lay down on the ice and grabbed Hansje by the hand. Someone else held that man by his feet and slowly pulled him back. Gradually, Hansje slid out of the water and lay on the ice.

"Get up, get up, quick!" the men shouted as they grabbed him, one by each arm and skated with him back to the safe end of the lake. They skated very fast, right into the icy north wind. Hansje was getting colder and colder. All he could think of was that now, for sure, he was going to get sick with pneumonia and die. He was crying because he didn't want to die.

When they got to the north end of the lake, the two men bent down and took their skates off and took Hansje's skates off and then grabbed him by the hands and ran with him towards a big house. By this time Hansje was very, very cold and shivering so hard he could hardly cry. When they got to the house, they pounded on the back door, and a lady let them into the kitchen.

They quickly took off his icy, wet clothes, everything from his icy wet jacket to his icy wet underwear. Then they quickly wrapped him in a warm, dry blanket, put him on a chair in front of the heater, and put his feet in a basin of warm water. Then they filled a small glass from a large brown bottle and made him drink it. It tasted awful, like really strong cough syrup, but it made him feel warm and tingly all over. "Drink some more," they said, "it is good for when you fall into icy water."

Hansje was still crying and asking the lady and the men, "Am I going to get sick with pneumonia and die? Am I going to get sick with pneumonia and die?"

"No, you won't get sick with pneumonia and die," the men said. "We got you out of the water right away and made you run and got your blood circulating. Now tell us your name and phone number."

And Hansje said, "Are you sure I won't get sick with pneumonia and die. My Mama always tells me not to get wet in the winter because I will get sick with pneumonia and die."

"No, you won't get sick and die," the men said again, "now tell us your name and phone number."

So Hansje said, "My name is Hansje, and the phone number is 7181, but are you sure I won't get sick with pneumonia and die?" He did listen to Mama after all. He sure knew what she had said about not getting wet and cold in winter because he would get sick with pneumonia and die.

One of the men phoned Mama and Papa and told them what had happened to their boy. They arrived after half an hour, bringing some dry clothes with them. The men who had pulled Hansje out of the water shook hands with Hansje's Mama and Papa. Then the lady who owned the house made them all sit around in that kitchen for another half an hour while Hansje warmed up some more. While waiting, they drank from small glasses of that awful tasting stuff that is good for you when you fall into the icy water and makes you feel all warm and tingly inside, even though none of them had fallen into the icy water.

Finally, Hansje got dressed in his dry clothes and walked home with Mama and Papa who kept telling him that he should not skate so fast that he couldn't see where he was going. And that he should have stayed where the other people were because it was dangerous to go where the ice was thin and where there were no people. And didn't he know that if he got wet in the winter, he would get sick with pneumonia and die?

But Hansje was thinking of how fun it was to skate so fast that he could hardly see where he was going. He also thought about how he got wetter and colder than he had ever been in his whole life, and how the men who pulled him out of the water were very sure that he would *not* get pneumonia and die.

So he thought, *Hmm, I wonder if my Mama is just trying to scare me by talking about me dying all the time.*

Did Hansje ever go skating that fast on a frozen lake again?

Of course, he did.

It takes more than falling into icy water, nearly drowning and, almost freezing, to stop a boy like Hansje from skating fast.

After all, he was Hansje, the boy who loved to go fast.

29 Hansje Takes Wobbie to Look at Trains

Hansje had a problem. He wanted to stay out of trouble, but he didn't want just to do boring things and miss out on exciting things. So, when he had to choose between doing a boring, but safe thing and an exciting, but dangerous thing, he usually chose to do the exciting, but dangerous thing. It's what nine-year-old boys like Hansje do.

One day, Mama said to him, "Hansje, please take Wobbie for a walk. He's getting in the way." Hansje said okay, because he was pretty obedient, even though he was very curious about a lot of things which often got him into trouble. So Hansje took his little brother Wobbie by the hand and off they went to look at the trains.

Mama was happy because Wobbie was always

getting in her way and with him gone, she finally had a chance to make lunch. But, if she had known what was going to happen on that walk, she probably wouldn't have been very happy at all.

Hansje decided to walk to the train tracks which were about four blocks from their house. On the way, Hansje met his friend Wim who asked, "Hey, where are you two going?"

"To the train yard!

"Okay, I'm coming too."

Little Wobbie couldn't walk very fast so it took a long time to get to the train yard. There were probably a dozen train tracks and several rows of boxcars and small train yard engines.

It was always fun to go there to watch. The train yard engines pushed the cars together and made trains out of them. Hansje liked to hear the clanging noise, and sometimes there was a little accident, and a boxcar would get stuck in a rail switch or even slip off the rails. That meant they had to bring a huge crane to lift it back on. Hansje and Wim both hoped that would happen because the trainmen would shout at each other and there would be lots of noise and excitement.

Of course, the boys couldn't just walk into the train yard; that would be very dangerous. You can imagine what would happen if kids could just go wandering around in the train yard looking at train cars while they were rolling this way and that way, being coupled together.

What if some kids started playing tag and one of them stumbled and fell, and a train car ran over his leg? You can imagine what would happen.

Since the people who built the train yard didn't want anything terrible like that to happen, they built a fence all along the track. That fence would keep everyone out. It wasn't the same kind of fence that is around schoolyards. Those are heavy wire fences.

This train yard fence was like a huge picket fence made out of long pieces of metal rod, like long broomsticks. The metal rods were fastened to long flat cross pieces. The rods were very tall, much higher than your head, and they were quite close together -- a cat could get between the rods but not a dog, maybe a puppy could.

Oh, and one more thing, the very top of the rod wasn't rounded or flat, it was pointy, like a spear or an arrow point. That was to keep people from climbing over the fence. With those points sticking up nobody wanted to climb over that train yard fence; you would rip your pants or get yourself stuck on those points, for sure.

When Hansje, Wobbie, and Wim arrived, they tried to look at the trains but they couldn't. There were trains all right; they could hear them and sort of see them between the bushes growing on the other side of the fence. It was summer, so the bushes were full of leaves and, of course, the boys couldn't see through those leaves. Fortunately, the bushes were not as tall as the fence, just a low hedge.

So, Wim climbed up the fence a little way until his head stuck up above the top of the fence and he could see everything. Hansje climbed up the fence too. It was a little hard because the toes of his shoes just barely fit between those rods to step on the flat cross pieces on the other side of the fence.

Hansje and Wim watched as the small yard engines put a train together. They got more excited as a huge, black locomotive came smoking and puffing up to back into the front end of the train. Bang! Clank! Click! Then, Choof! Choof!, off it went.

Suddenly Hansje and Wim heard some whining and crying down below. Now what? Oh, of course, it was little Wobbie. He couldn't see a thing. Hansje climbed down and lifted Wobbie up, so his head stuck up above the fence so that he could see over the hedge.

"Hold on tight!" he said, and Wobbie held on tight.

His little shoes fit right between the rods so he could easily step on those flat pieces on the other side of the fence. Then Hansje climbed up alongside Wobbie and all three of the boys enjoyed the train show in the train yard for quite a while.

A big locomotive had just gone puffing, steaming and clanking by, shaking the ground and even the fence they were clinging to when Hansje thought he heard a strange sound. It sounded as if someone was trying to yell with his mouth full of something. He looked over at Wim and nearly fell off the fence in surprise and shock.

Wim's foot had skidded off the little flat cross piece and he had slipped down. One of those sharp pointy fence rods had speared him right under his chin and the point stuck up inside his mouth. That's why he couldn't yell very well!

Wim quickly put his foot back on the cross piece and lifted himself off the sharp point. He climbed down with blood streaming out of a nasty hole in the bottom of his chin. He was crying, spitting blood, and saying, "Ged downg, ged downg."

While Hansje was carefully climbing down, Wim did a very good thing. He reached up and lifted Wobbie off the fence and set him down on the ground. Then he ran home bleeding and crying and saying, "Owg, owg, id huds! Id huds." He couldn't talk very clearly with a hole in the bottom of his mouth.

While Hansje and Wobbie walked home, Hansje thought about Wim and hoped that God would look after him. He also wondered if he should tell Mama what had happened to Wim. He thought about it and realized Wobbie was too little to tell Mama what had happened. He also thought about how he loved Mama very much and didn't want her to worry. He also thought she just might worry if she knew what had happened, so, out of love for Mama, Hansje decided not to say anything about what happened.

When they got home, they were just in time for lunch. As they were sitting down at the table, Wobbie opened his mouth, stuck out his tongue, and said, "Id huds, id huds" but no one took any notice of him.

Good thing, too. This time, Hansje escaped getting into trouble.

In the fall, after the leaves were off the bushes and they didn't have to climb on the fence to see the trains, Hansje and Wobbie often went to the train yard. Wim came, too; he was quite proud of the scar under his chin. It was even bigger than the scar on Hansje's hand.

30 Hansje Smokes a Cigar

When Hansje had his tenth birthday, he felt so grown-up that he wanted to do more things that grown-up people did. He often wondered what it would feel like to be a real grown-up, to shave his beard and smoke cigars as Papa did.

He was, of course, already doing some things that grown-ups do. He also looked after his little sister Jannie and little brother Wobbie. Mostly, he took them for walks around the block or to the bakery to buy bread or the butcher shop to get meat for Mama. He sometimes took Wobbie to the train yard to look at trains, but Jannie didn't like going there. "Too noisy," she said.

He also delivered small packages of codfish, herring, or shrimp to customers and had them sign the bill which he never lost but always carefully brought back to Papa. And he helped Papa take the guts out of small fish, cutting off their fins and heads and then, very carefully, slicing the bones out. He did piles and piles of them after school and in the afternoons on Wednesday and Saturday when there was no school.

He was even in charge of the two giant, square vats of boiling oil where he fried the herring he had cleaned. He was good at it. One day his little sister Jannie came to watch him. She was way too little to help, so he told her to stand off to one side just in case the boiling oil splashed a bit.

He told her exactly what she would do someday when she was old enough. "Look", he said, "You hold each fresh herring by the tail and drag it back and forth in a pan of flour until it has flour all over it on both sides; then you lay it carefully on the rack, close to the other ones, but not touching."

When the whole rack was full, he called Papa, who came from the front of the store and lowered it into the boiling oil since it was too heavy and dangerous for Hansje to do by himself. After Papa had left, Hansje continued to teach his little sister Jannie.

"Now you have to watch for the herring to start floating to the top. When one floats, like this one, you scoop it out quickly with this wire mesh scoop and lay it on the drain rack, or it will burn. But while you watch for herring to start floating at the top, you have to keep flouring more herring and laying them on the second rack."

After he had filled that rack and all the first batch of herring had floated to the top and were safely on the drying rack, he called Papa who lowered the second rack into the second tank of boiling oil and carried the fried herring to the front of the store to sell them.

Of course, Jannie soon got bored and went back to the house in front of the store, but Hansje kept working for another hour, often with both racks in the boiling oil at the same time until he ran out of cleaned and deboned herring. When there were many customers, he turned down the burners under the oil pans and started all over again cleaning and de-boning herring.

Even though Hansje was doing all these grown-up things, they were never enough for him. He was always curious and looking to do something new, something he had never done before. There was one thing, in particular, he always wished he could try, but he was very sure Mama and Papa didn't want him to try it. He wanted to do it, anyway.

In those days, all the men smoked cigarettes and some of the women, too. Except on Sundays and other special days—then the men would smoke large brown cigars. On Sundays, after they had all walked back from church, and before they sat down to have lunch, Hansje liked to sit close to Papa or his uncles and smell their cigars before they lit them. They smelled pleasant, and all the cigars had nice coloured bands around them to tell what brand they were. Those bands were so beautiful. They had gold, red, and blue colors and pictures of men with large black beards and moustaches, with strange names like Don Alfredo, Ernst Casimir, and Willem II.

After Hansje had his tenth birthday, he wanted to smoke, and not just a cigarette. Oh no, that was for ordinary days. He wanted to smoke a cigar.

Some of his uncles had given him dimes for his birthday. Usually, he went to the ice cream shop and bought an ice cream sandwich. In those long-ago days, they didn't have ice cream cones, but they took a thin wafer cookie and smeared some ice cream on it, then they put another cookie on top, squeezed it together, and scraped the leftover ice cream from the edges. Hansje loved to buy and eat ice cream sandwiches with his birthday dimes. But this time he was so very curious about smoking a cigar that he decided to use one of his dimes to buy a cigar and smoke it.

So, he walked into the cigar shop and laid his dime on the counter and said, "I want a ten-cent cigar, please."

The clerk looked in a couple of boxes and finally found his cheapest cigar. He wrapped it up in paper and gave it to Hansje, who carefully put it into his pocket and walked home. Now, when and where was he going to smoke it?

Hmm, he hadn't thought that far ahead. Maybe next Saturday afternoon, after he finished frying fish and delivered the packages of fish on his bike, he could take his cigar and a box of matches with him. Then when he was done, he could pedal his bike to a park and sit someplace where no one could see him, light up his cigar, and have his first smoke.

That was a great plan. But where was he going to keep his cigar in the meantime? He couldn't bring it into the house because Mama was always cleaning and she would find it for sure. Besides, his little sister Jannie and even littler brother Wobbie were always rummaging through all his things and might find it. He couldn't even hide it under his mattress because he never knew when Mama would tear off all the sheets to wash them and flip the mattress over to air it out. She was always cleaning up and washing stuff.

So, he had to find a place outside the house. And the sooner, the better. He walked through the front gate and went directly to the side of the front room windows where the drain spout came down from the roof and carefully tucked his paper wrapped cigar behind the spout as high as he could reach. He stepped back—there, perfect. The bushes covered it. You couldn't see unless you knew where to look. And it was nice and dry. He could hardly wait until delivery time late Saturday afternoon!

That Saturday, right after lunch, while Hansje was frying those herring in the boiling oil, he just kept thinking how neat it was going to be to smoke a cigar and finally be a grown-up. He was calling Papa to tell him the last batch of herring was floured and ready to put in the boiling oil when he heard voices in the store. Voices that weren't talking about fish, but about cigars. Oh no! Now what?

When Papa came in to put the last tray of herring into the boiling oil he said, "Hansje, come with me." He didn't put the tray in the oil but just left it sitting there. When Hansje walked into the store behind Papa, he saw two things. One was the old man who came to help weed the little garden in front of the house, and the other thing was what both the old man and Papa were looking at. His cigar!

Oh, why hadn't he remembered that old man who sometimes came around on Saturday right after lunch to weed the garden? Of course, when trimming the bushes, he would see that wrapped cigar behind the drain spout. Hansje's bottom could already feel the whack, whack, whack of the spanking with the cane carpet beater that he just knew he was going to get. Papa turned to him and asked, "Hansje, is that cigar yours?"

"Yes, Papa," he whispered.

"When were you going to smoke it?" Papa asked.

"This afternoon, after the deliveries."

"But Hansje, Saturday is not a good day for smoking cigars. Tomorrow, after church, we will smoke our cigars together."

Hansje couldn't believe his ears! What? No spanking with the carpet beater? Wow, what a relief!

The next day was Sunday and Hansje could hardly sit still through the church service; he was so excited about smoking cigars with Papa after church. When they got home, Mama started making lunch and Papa said,

"I'm going for a walk around the block with Hansje to smoke our cigars." She looked at him with a little frown but didn't say anything.

Papa went into his office, got himself a cigar, and lit it. Then he took Hansje's cigar and lit it for him. It was a cheap cigar and didn't want to light very well, so Papa had to light it several times with the flame of the kitchen gas stove, but finally, it stayed lit, and they both walked out the door. Hansje took a puff and coughed a bit, but held the cigar between his thumb and two fingers just as Papa did. Whenever Papa took a puff, he did, too.

After a while, he stopped coughing and kept puffing on his cigar until he started feeling a bit woozy. He felt a little like that time he was on a boat on the trip to Friesland when he was only seven. They were about half way around the block, and Papa had to keep saying,

"You have to keep puffing on your cigar, or it will go out."

As he did, he felt sweaty, dizzy, and more and more seasick, just like he was on that nasty boat trip. He couldn't wait to get home, throw away his cigar, and lie down. Just as they arrived at the front gate of the garden, he leaned over the fence and puked and puked. He dropped his cigar and didn't pick it up again.

He held Papa's hand as they walked up the path and into the house. Then he went into the kitchen and rinsed out his mouth with some water. Mama said, "Okay, lunch is ready."

But Hansje didn't feel like eating. Instead, he just wanted to lie down on the couch for a while, which he did. He could hear Mama talk loudly to Papa in her scolding voice. "You shouldn't have done that," she said, "look how sick that cigar made him!"

And then Papa said in a softer voice, "That's true. But now he probably won't start smoking for a long time. He may have learned his lesson."

Well, that was true. Hansje was not curious about smoking anymore. He never smoked a cigar again. When he was much older, he tried smoking a cigarette once to impress some girls, but he started feeling the same yucky way he did that time with the cigar, so he stopped. The girls laughed at him, but he didn't care.

Hansje still liked doing grown-up things, but he never tried to smoke again.

And about ten years later, Papa decided that smoking wasn't good for his body, so he wanted to stop smoking, too. It took a long time. He had to pray to God a lot to help him quit. Then Hansje realized that *not* smoking was, even more, a grownup thing to do than smoking.

31 Hansje Runs a Foot Race

When Hansje was ten years old, his school organized a special sports day with another school. The afternoon of the sports day all the students, their teachers, and some parents came together on a big, open field and the students had races. Hansje was excited since he was a pretty good runner, probably because he was always playing tag and that means lots of running.

First, everybody ran about 50 metres which is not a long distance, but it showed who could sprint fast and Hansje did quite well. Then the sports organizer said,

"Now we are going to run the 100 metre races. The first ones to run are Hansje and Piet. Please come to the starting line."

So Hansje went to the start line and a boy from another school the same age, but a little taller than Hansje walked up too. They stood along the starting line, and the organizer counted, "One, two, three. Go!"

Both boys started off together, then slowly Hansje got a little ahead, and he felt he might win. But then Piet came level with him, and no matter how hard Hansje pumped his legs he couldn't keep up with Piet. Soon, Piet was two metres ahead. Then, just before they got to the big tree which was the end of the race, a very strange thing happened.

Piet suddenly fell over backward. As Hansje turned his head to look, something zipped by just over his head.

When he reached the big tree, he turned and jogged back to where Piet was lying and saw a long wire stretched tight between two posts, like a tall fence with only one wire. That's what Piet had run into, and that's what had zipped over Hansje's head when he turned to look back at Piet.

By this time parents and teachers had come running up. He heard somebody say, "The wire hit him right in the throat. He can't talk. Quick. Take him to a hospital!"

And someone else shouted, "Why is this wire stretched here? Are they putting up a fence?"

There was a lot of confusion; the announcer canceled the race, and someone came to see if Hansje was okay. He was, the wire had just grazed the top of his head. It was a little scraped and sore, but it was not a problem.

Poor Piet, however, had to be in the hospital for a long time and had to have surgery to fix his throat so he could talk again.

Hansje was very thankful that he was a little shorter and slower than Piet, because, otherwise, that wire might have hit *him* in the throat. He would have hated not being able to talk very well since he loved telling stories to his friends. That night in bed, he not only prayed for Piet, but he thanked God that he was shorter and slower than Piet.

From then on Hansje didn't like sports days very much.

32 Hansje Proves He Can Swim

Summer holidays are usually a lot of fun, but not in Holland in the city where Hansje lived when he was in elementary school. Instead of being two months long, they lasted only half a month. And none of the school had playgrounds or play equipment near them. So, during the two weeks of summer holidays, all Hansje could do was play in the street. Roll marbles in the gutter along the curb, or ride his bike, or kick a ball on the street with his friends, always watching out, so they didn't get run over by a car.

Then, one day just after the summer holidays started, Mama said, "Hansje, tomorrow you get to visit your cousins in Baarn for six days."

Wow! Hansje was excited to go to his cousins in the little town of Baarn because he had never visited them for an overnight before. In fact, he had never been away from home by himself for an overnight visit.

Mama smiled to see him so happy. But if she had known what Hansje was going to be doing during those days, maybe she would not have smiled.

The next day Papa took Hansje to Baarn and dropped him off at the cousins' house. Hansje's aunt and uncle came out to welcome him, and his three boy cousins crowded around him to show him where he would be sleeping.

That night, as Hansje was lying in a strange bed, trying to fall asleep, he felt very lonely. Even though he was already ten years old, he even felt like crying a little bit. But then he said his bedtime prayer and added a little piece.

"And please, dear Lord, look after me during this time I am so far away from home."

Then he wondered what kind of fun he was going to have with his older cousins the next day. That made him feel much better, and he fell asleep right away.

The next day, after breakfast, the three cousins made some sandwiches, put them into a bag, and the four of them went for a long hike. Hansje didn't know anything about hiking in the fields and forest because he only ever walked on streets and sidewalks.

After a few minutes of following a sandy path, they started tromping about among the bushes. Suddenly Hansje stumbled and fell. His cousins laughed and shouted, "Hey, watch out for the rabbit holes!"

But a little later Hansje was in trouble again when he lagged behind his cousins and tried to take a shortcut through some tall grass. Suddenly he got his shoes all wet, and the cousins called out, "Hey, dummy, that's a swamp. Get out of there!"

Hansje didn't know anything about rabbit holes or swamps. He only knew the city and how to look out for traffic. But that didn't help him out here. He felt dumb, but he hated being called a dummy. That afternoon they went to dig in sand pits, but again, they kept telling him what he should do, because they knew all about digging in sandpits and Hansje didn't know anything other than the sandbox his little brother Wobbie played in. Yes, he felt like a dummy who didn't know anything.

But the next day when they told Hansje he should put on his swimsuit he got excited. When Hansje was very little, he learned how to swim, mostly by lying on his stomach on a chair and moving his arms and his legs, pretending to swim. He also practiced holding his breath for as long as he could.

When he was a little older, he got to make those same motions with his arms and legs in the water, and presto! He was swimming! From then on, every Saturday afternoon, he walked to the indoor swimming pool to swim and dive for a whole hour with his friends.

Hansje and his cousins put on their swimsuits, took some towels, and walked down the block, around the corner, and through a field to the edge of the river. When they got to the river, he got even more excited. He had only ever swum in a swimming pool before, never in a river or a lake.

At first, he was a little afraid to go into the river. The water looked dark, not nice, clear, and clean like in a swimming pool. When he swam down towards the bottom, it was all dark; the only light came from the surface. Then he felt mud, not shiny, clean white tiles. But he got used to the river pretty quickly.

They played tag in the water and tried to keep up with sailboats and rowboats that went by. Once in a while, a bigger boat would come by, and they bounced around in the waves that it made. The next day they went again, and the day after that too. Hansje got braver and braver.

One day, one of the older cousins said, "Hey, let's have a contest to see who can stay under water the longest."

He said that because he was the oldest and he always won that contest. Hansje and his three cousins all lined up on the bank of the river and took some deep breaths. Then they all dove in at once. Of course, everyone knows that the only way to win a contest like that is to cheat.

You dive down, but soon you come up for air and dive back down again. As long as no one else is coming up for air at the same time and sees you, you can keep doing that for a long time.

But Hansje thought of something different. Instead of diving down to the muddy bottom and then coming back up to take a cheating breath, he dove in and swam underwater all the way to the other side of the river. When he felt the reeds and bushes of the other side, he very quietly and carefully, stuck his head out of the water and took a breath.

Then he went under water again and wriggled himself further into the reeds and kept his eyes and nose above water to breathe and to look. He watched from his hiding place as first one cousin popped up and dove back down, and then another cousin popped up and dove again. Such cheaters!

But soon two cousins' heads popped up at the same time, so they caught each other and had to stay up. Then the third cousin popped up to breathe. Then Hansje watched as all three of them talked a bit together and took breaths and dove down again. Those cheaters! All three were getting together to cheat against him. That sure wasn't fair!

Hansje sat quietly in the reeds way over on the far side of the river until all three cousins popped back up again. This time, he could see they were getting a little worried. He could see them talk to each other; then they climbed onto the river bank and started walking along it, looking down into the water.

OK, now it was Hansje's turn. He took a very deep breath, slid quietly under the water, and swam like crazy back to the other side of the river. There he popped up, breathing hard, and gasping, "Who won? Who won?"

The three cousins looked at each other and wondered, but they never guessed that he had been all the way across the river and hiding in the reeds. They knew Hansje had cheated somehow, but they didn't know how he had done it.

They kept asking, but he just acted mysteriously and then said, "Hey, look, there is a row boat coming, let's dive under it and come up on the other side!"

That was a favourite game, and soon they were

diving underneath the rowboats and canoes going by. Of course, you couldn't dive underneath a sailboat because it has a long keel board sticking way down into the water to keep the sailboat from tipping over when the wind blows, and they go fast, so the keel board might whack you as you swim underneath.

Suddenly, they heard a big boat coming up the river. It was a long freight barge, flat bottomed with a strong motor and a big propeller, called a screw, at the back.

Then Hansje said something that, if Mama had heard, would make her quit smiling and start frowning. "Let's dive underneath this barge," he said, "and come up on the other side."

The other cousins looked at him with strange looks and said things like, "Are you crazy? You could never swim that far."

"You must be nuts. You can't go that deep."

"That big screw will chop you up."

They also said, "Don't do it!"

But Hansje didn't just sit there on the side of the river and watch that long barge slowly go by. No, he was remembering how his cousins had been making him feel like a dummy, who couldn't do anything right in the fields and forest, and now he thought he could show them he could do something that they couldn't do.

So he took a very, very deep breath and dove in. As he did, the captain of the boat was yelling at him to get away from the barge. But he never heard that. He was swimming for his life. He was smart, of course, because he dove in while the barge was still churning along slowly so that when he went underneath, it was just the narrow front part of the boat that was above him, not the wide middle part with that horribly dangerous, churning screw right behind.

He sensed the huge black bulk of the barge above him and heard the thump, Thump, THUMP! of the big motor. But above all, he heard the chush! Chush! CHUSH! of that mighty screw getting closer. He swam deep and hard and wondered if he would feel the muddy bottom sliding along his stomach.

When he looked up ahead and saw daylight on the surface, he shot up and popped up out of the water, flipped to his back, and kept swimming away from the barge. The captain was leaning over the side of the boat, looking very angry, shaking both his fists and shouting many words that Hansje had never heard or read before.

When the barge was gone, Hansje calmly swam back to his cousins, climbed out of the river, and sat there resting for awhile. His cousins didn't know what to say, so they didn't say anything. From the looks on their faces, Hansje could see that they thought he was crazy to do a thing like that, but he also thought they might be respecting him a little more. After all, none of them had ever done something like that. And, best of all, from then on, they never again called him a dummy anymore.

33 Hansje Finds a Way into the Swimming Pool

One day Hansje and his bigger cousins were swimming and diving along the bank of the river when they heard some laughing and shouting in the distance. Hansje asked his cousins what it was.

The youngest cousin said, "It's a swimming pool, right next to the river."

So Hansje asked, "How come people need a swimming pool when there is a whole river to swim in?"

"Because it has lots of slides, diving boards, and rubber rafts to float on. We like going in there because you can slide, dive, and play tag with other kids."

"Well, let's go there," Hansje said. "It sounds like fun."

"We can't," the oldest cousin said, "they won't let you in unless you pay. There's a wall all the way around the pool, and you can only get in through the door on the street side.

And, of course, they didn't have money. But Hansje still wanted to see what that swimming pool was like, so they all walked along the bank until they got to a high wooden wall. The wall went all the way from the street right down to the river and down into the water right around the whole swimming pool. From behind the wall, they could hear kids splashing and laughing.

Hansje jumped into the river and swam along the wall. He could see that the wall wasn't solid on the side of the water at all. It was more like a giant picket fence. The upright planks were bolted to cross beams which were bolted to big posts that stuck way down into the bottom of the river. The big planks were not tight together; they were far enough apart so that fresh river water could flow into the swimming pool, but not far enough apart that anyone could squeeze between them to get in.

The more Hansje peered between the planks at the kids having fun on the slides, diving boards, and big rafts, the more he wanted to get in. Suddenly, he had an idea. He took a deep breath and dove down feeling the upright plank with his hands. At the bottom of the plank, he got to the mud of the river. The plank next to it went right down into the mud, too. He kept coming up for air and then diving down to check out a few more planks. Then he found what he was hoping to find.

He came up smiling because what he found would remind his cousins he might be younger than they were but he was braver and could swim better than they could. He took another deep breath and dove down to the bottom of the last plank he had checked. It was rotten and had broken off a couple of feet above the mud. Hansje wriggled himself through the hole and came up again, this time on the inside of the plank fence.

"This plank is broken off at the bottom," he said, "you can crawl underneath it." Of course, he was only ten years old and smaller than his cousins, so it was easier for him. They dove down one by one and came up on the inside, too, looking a little scared but excited at the same time.

A few minutes later they were all sliding down the slides, diving off the diving boards, and playing tag over and under the rubber rafts with the cousins' friends. Later that day when the swimming pool closed, they were the only ones to walk out through the door onto the street wearing only their swimming trunks and not even carrying towels. They had all been pretty scared wiggling through the hole at the bottom of that rotted plank, way under the water, in the mud, and in the dark. They came in that way, but it was so scary they didn't want to go out that way. The manager looked at them suspiciously, probably guessing how they got in, but it was too late then.

They walked back to where they had left their clothes on the river bank, put them on, and walked home for supper.

"So, did you have a good time swimming today?" Hansje's aunt asked.

"Oh, yes, Auntie, we had a really good time," Hansje answered.

"Good, I'll phone your Mama and tell her all about it tonight," she said.

But Hansje thought, *No you won't. You won't tell her ALL about it because you don't know the HALF of what we did.*

He loved Papa and Mama so much he didn't want them to worry about him. That's why he didn't explain anything to his auntie. Of course, there was also the chance he would have been taken home immediately for a meeting with Mama and Papa and the carpet beater.

He also felt a little guilty when he said his bedtime prayer. He had been so excited about finding a way into that play area through the hole under the fence; he forgot it was sort of like stealing. Four kids got in without paying the admission, which he knew was cheating. He didn't know what to say to God about that, so he didn't say anything, but decided he would never do that again.

34 Hansje Cheats on an Arithmetic Test

Hansje liked studying many things at school. He loved maps and reading about faraway lands or long ago times. He loved reading all kinds of books. But there were some studies in school that he did not like. One of them was math. He hated everything about numbers. Adding and subtracting them. Multiplying and dividing them. Doing fractions and percentages.

He especially hated memorizing multiplication tables, and everyone knows that by fifth grade, students need to know the multiplication tables all the way up to 12. That's 120 number facts, and Hansje knew only about half that many.

He spent a lot of time memorizing them. Whenever he did something wrong in school, like come late, or talk without putting up his hand, the teacher made him stay in at recess or after school and write out multiplication tables. So he studied lots, but still got many answers wrong in class. Other kids often laughed at him when he gave the wrong answer, but not his teacher. His grade five teacher was a big, strong man who frowned at him and looked angry. Tests were the worst. Hansje just knew he would usually get the wrong answer in math problems and he always got the worst mark in the class.

Hansje felt so bad about being such a number dummy that he finally decided to cheat. He knew cheating was a bad thing to do, but it was also easy to do. His school had double desks in some classrooms, which meant that two people sat side by side at the same school desk. So, sitting right next to someone else made it easy to sneak a quick peek at their test paper and copy their answer. Hansje sat right next to Henk who was good at math. He sometimes got a few answers wrong, but nothing like Hansje who got almost every answer wrong. So whenever they had a test, Hansje cheated and copied some answers from Hank's paper, when neither Hank nor the teacher was looking.

That worked pretty well, and Hansje no longer was the worst in the class. But then, one Friday there was a special math test. It was an important one, and the teacher had prepared two tests. One for the person sitting on the left side of the desk and one for the person on the right side of the desk. But the teacher didn't tell anybody that.

So just like all other times, Hansje tried to work out some problems, but they were way too hard for him. By the time he repeated a multiplication in his mind to get an answer for one part of the problem, he had forgotten what the other part of the problem was. So he did as he always did and started copying answers from Henk's test paper.

Then, just before the end of the class, the teacher said, "Oh, by the way, those of you on the left side of the desk have a different test than those of you on the right side."

"What?! Oh no!"

Hansje knew he was in terrible trouble. The teacher would know for sure that he was cheating. Hansje was so afraid of being found out, he quickly erased every answer on his test paper. Then he just wrote down some numbers, any kind of numbers. Just as he finished scribbling in a number for the last problem, the teacher said, "Okay, stop and pass your test papers to the front."

As Hansje left the classroom, he knew that the teacher would see that all of Hansje's answers were wrong, but he hoped that he would not suspect him of trying to cheat since at least Hansje's answers wouldn't be the same as Henk's.

On Monday, however, things did not turn out well for Hansje. First, the teacher read everyone's mark starting with the person who got the highest mark. Hansje's name was, of course, at the bottom of the list. He put the paper on his desk, turned to the blackboard and picked up his metre-long round rod that he used to point things out on maps. He looked at Hansje and said, "Hansje, come here."

Hansje walked slowly to the front of the class to where the teacher stood waiting with his rod. The entire class was silent, staring, hardly daring to breathe. Hansje's hands shook, his lips trembled, and his eyes filled with tears. The teacher didn't say a word, but just grabbed Hansje by the back of his collar and pushed him down to the floor. He clamped Hansje's head tightly between his knees, grabbed his belt, and pulled up so that Hansje's bottom stuck out facing the whole class.

Then Whack! Whack! Whack! He beat Hansje's poor bottom with his rod, over and over again. Hansje screamed and howled. Whack! Whack! Whack! When the teacher finally stopped thrashing him and let go of Hansje's belt, Hansje fell to the floor crying.

"Go to your desk!" the teacher shouted. Hansje got up and stumbled past the other students and sat at his desk. He leaned forward on his elbows all the rest of the class time because he couldn't sit very well. It stung and hurt for a long time. He was still very sore that night, but he didn't tell Papa or Mama because he was afraid he would have gotten another spanking with the carpet beater.

That night, after his bedtime prayer, he told God he was sorry he had cheated when he knew that was the wrong thing to do. He decided never to cheat again. He also asked God to make him smart in math. Or if not, then at least make him smart in something else in school.

God answered some of his prayers. He helped Hansje never to cheat again and He made Hansje smart in reading and writing stories. But Hansje never got smart in math. Even five years later when he was in tenth grade in Canada, sitting right there in class, he cried silently, hiding behind his hands, because he couldn't understand algebra.

35 Hansje Stands Up for Wobbie

Hansje walked to school every day. He walked one block to the corner of the street where he lived. Then he walked two short blocks and crossed a wide road. Then he walked a long block to get to the big main street where there was a huge church with a very tall square tower. About ten stories up were four giant clocks, one on each of the four sides. And above the clocks was a tall, pointy tower called a spire. Once Hansje got to the big church, he knew it was only three more blocks to his school.

Every morning Hansje walked seven blocks to school, and every noon he walked back home for lunch. Then he walked back to school again, and after school was out, he walked back home again. He was ten years old and in fifth grade, and he had been doing that ever since first grade.

Hansje's little brother Wobbie went to school, too. But he just went to Kindergarten in the mornings because he was only four. So every morning Hansje and his little sister Jannie took their little brother Wobbie by the hand and walked those seven blocks to school with him, and at noon Hansje took him by the hand again and took him home for lunch. Then in the afternoon, Jannie would play with her friends, and Hansje could finally run and play with his friends on the way home from school without having to look after Wobbie.

One day, at lunch time, Hansje and Wobbie were walking in the schoolyard and were just about to turn the corner onto the sidewalk when --

Swish, Whack!

Swish, Whack!

Waaaahhh!!

What was that?

Hansje yanked Wobbie away from the fence and saw a boy with a long, thin stick. He was laughing and trying to hit Wobbie with it again. That was the Swish, Whack! part.

The Waaaaahhh!! part was, of course, Wobbie screaming in fright and crying in pain.

Hansje looked at his little brother and saw two red stripes right on his cheek. That nasty boy had hit his little brother right in the face.

Well, Hansje didn't like that one little bit! He felt like grabbing the boy by the shirt, dragging him over the fence, and beating him up. But, of course, he knew he should not do that. Mama had told him many,

many times that he should never fight, and that if a boy did something bad to him, Hansje should tell some adult and not just hit back.

So Hansje walked down the sidewalk with Wobbie until he came to a gate into the yard where the boy with the long whippy stick lived. As soon as the boy saw them come into the yard, he ran to hide around the back of the house.

Then Hansje, the boy who loved to do adult things, walked up to the front door of the house and knocked loudly. A man opened the door and shouted,

"What do you want?!!"

Hansje politely said,

"Excuse me sir, but a boy in this yard hit my little brother on the side of the face with a stick and left those red marks. See?" he said, pointing to Wobbie who was still sniffling.

The man didn't even look. He just shouted some very nasty words. Yes, swear words that people should never say, especially to kids, and especially to such a good, brave boy as Hansje.

Then he slammed the door shut and left Hansje and Wobbie standing there. The bad boy with the stick poked his head around the corner of the house and stuck out his tongue at Hansje. But Hansje just said, "Let's go," and walked out of the yard and down the block.

Hansje looked calm on the outside, but on the inside, he was really angry. First, that nasty boy had hit his little brother for no reason at all. Then a horrible man had cursed him with terrible swear words and slammed the door right in his face, and then the nasty boy stuck out his tongue at them.

He thought about how some people in the Bible could pray and ask God to do terrible things to their enemies, and he sort of wondered if he should do that. But after a while, he started thinking about how they would soon be home and would eat a nice lunch, and he started to forget about the mean boy and the nasty man. Hansje and Wobbie were just walking along the sidewalk in front of that giant church with the tall clock tower when something very unexpected happened.

First, Hansje heard someone running behind him. Then he heard some terrible swear words, and, just as he was going to turn around and see who was saying those terrible words, he felt a very hard kick on his bottom, flew through the air and landed on his face and stomach on the sidewalk. Poor little Wobbie didn't know what to think, and so he just started crying again. Waaah!

As Hansje got to his knees, he turned and saw the horrible man who had slammed the door in his face, walking away, looking over his shoulder and laughing. When Hansje got up he rubbed his bottom; it was very sore from being kicked so hard.

But Hansje knew what to do; he walked straight home. Well, not quite straight, because it was a little hard to walk straight with such a sore bottom. But when he got home, he told Mama the whole story. When Papa came in for lunch, Mama told him the whole story. Then Papa made Hansje tell the whole story to him. They asked Wobbie, but he was only four and was too little to tell very much. But the two red stripes on his cheek were still there, so they knew that part was true.

Then Papa picked up the telephone, called the police station, and talked to a policeman. And after lunch, Hansje and Papa walked to the police station which was right across the road from the big church with the clock tower. There Hansje had to tell the whole story to the policeman. After writing down some notes, the policeman told Hansje and Papa to wait.

After a long wait, the policeman walked back into the room. With him was the horrible man who liked to swear at little boys, slam doors in their faces, chase after them, and kick. But this time he wasn't swearing, or slamming doors, or chasing, or kicking anyone. He stood very quietly beside the policeman and looked down at the floor.

The policeman and Hansje's Papa talked together for a long time. Then the policeman talked to the nasty man, and then the man came up to Hansje and said very quietly, without shouting or using any bad words, "I'm sorry for kicking you, and I'm sorry for swearing at you, and I'm sorry that my son hit your little brother."

Then the policeman wrote on a paper and kept part for himself and the other part he gave to the man and said, "If you ever do anything like this again in your whole life, you are going to jail."

Then the man left, and the policeman said to

Hansje's Papa, "You did the right thing by coming here and telling me all about this. And you did the right thing when you taught your boy not to fight or hit back when something bad happens, but to find an adult to tell about it."

Then he shook hands with Papa, and he shook hands with Hansje and said,

"I hope that if I ever have a little boy of my own, he will be just as brave as you and care for his little brother just like you did."

Then the doors opened, and all the other policemen came running in carrying pails of ice cream with big bowls and spoons for everyone, and jumped up on the tables and started singing and dancing, and . . . Or maybe not.

But for a long time, whenever Hansje walked home past the front of the giant church, he looked over his shoulder to make sure there wasn't someone running up behind him to kick him on the bottom.

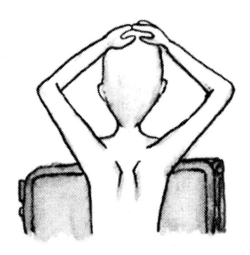

36 Hansje Learns About Emigration

When Hansje was eleven years old, Mama was very sad. Her sister, Hansje's Auntie Anna, her husband Gabe and their two children were moving far away.

Mama sobbed as she hugged her sister in farewell, "You are emigrating to Canada, to live there forever, and I'll never see you again." Papa shook hands hard and long with Uncle Gabe and wished him well. And Hansje and his seven-year-old sister Jannie said goodbye to their two cousins, Jannie and Sydney.

Everyone kept saying, "We'll never see you again, but we'll write often."

It turned out that the last part was true. They did write often, but the first part wasn't true. They surely *did* see each other again, a lot. Even more, than they ever had before.

Here's what happened.

Papa didn't talk to Hansje about adult things like business, making money, and paying bills, but Hansje wasn't dumb. He learned a lot by keeping his eyes and ears open when he was around his parents.

He had figured out that things were not going very well for Papa's fish selling business. Every morning when Hansje got up to have breakfast and walk to school, Papa was already cleaning fish in the fish store behind the house After supper, Papa used to sit in his chair and read the paper, but now he went back to working in his shop. And Hansje helped a lot, too. He made deliveries on his bike; he gutted fish, deep-fried the herring, and he cleaned up the shop. Sometimes he even helped customers and wrapped their fish for them.

"I'm selling three times as much fish as before the war," he heard Papa tell Mama one Sunday afternoon when they thought he was reading a book and not listening to them, "We should be getting richer, but we are getting poorer. It's all those taxes!"

Hansje knew about taxes. There were all sorts of reasons and ways in which the government made people pay taxes. And after you paid taxes, you didn't have money for things like toys, or nice clothes or a bigger bike. Papa hated to pay taxes, but there was no way anyone could get out of paying them. So Papa just worked harder to sell more fish and earn more money.

On another Sunday afternoon, Hansje was quietly sitting in the corner of the living room reading a book when three of his uncles came to visit. Mama and the aunts all went into another room while Papa and his three brothers stayed in the room where Hansje was reading. They were all in the fish selling business. They poured themselves some coffee, then they lit up cigars, and Hansje almost got up to ask if he could have the little bands around the cigars because he had a collection. But then he decided just to keep quiet and sit where he was. He thought he might hear something interesting. And he did. He still was looking at his book and turning pages, but he wasn't reading. Instead, he was listening very carefully.

They kept talking about the government wanting ordinary one-man businesses like the one Papa had, to sell their businesses to large companies and just go to work for them. None of the uncles liked that idea. They wanted to keep on being their own boss just like Papa. But the government charged smaller businesses much more tax than bigger businesses so that it got harder and harder to run a small business.

Then they started talking about some other business friends who were emigrating. Hansje knew very well that meant moving far away to Canada, like Mama's sister Anna had done with her family, or her sister Klaske's family who emigrated to Australia, or her sister Siep's family who went to the United States.

Suddenly, he heard something so exciting; he almost dropped his book.

"I'd like to emigrate too," Papa said, "Gabe and Anna keep writing to tell me Canada is a great country with lots of jobs and opportunities to start a business and that I should come. Aaltje and I have been praying about it, and one evening as we were reading the Bible we came to Genesis 12:1. It was God speaking to Abram, but it sounded to Aaltje and me as if God was speaking to us, 'Go from your country, your people and your father's household to the land I will show you.'"

The uncles all nodded very seriously and looked as if this decision was not a surprise to them. Then Papa continued, "I told Gabe and Anna that although I'd love to emigrate, it would not be as easy for us as it had been for them."

As Papa and the uncles kept talking Hansje listened carefully and learned that there were two kinds of people emigrating. Holland had too many people, not enough houses, and not enough jobs. If you were just an unskilled labourer, without much schooling, the government would pay you to leave. That's how Uncle Gabe and untie Anna and their family, and the other aunts and their families could leave. The government paid their boat tickets so they would go away and make more room. But people who had their own business and were taxpayers were different. They had to pay their own tickets. And the government didn't want them to leave, so they made emigrating very difficult for those people.

When Hansje turned twelve years old, it was no secret anymore. Hansje's family were definitely emigrating to Canada! Hansje was excited to go, even though it meant leaving all his school friends. He wasn't afraid of learning a new language, nor was he afraid of Canadian snow or ice. He didn't know exactly what part of Canada they were going to, but he studied the map of Canada carefully, imagining himself swimming in some of the lakes he saw on the map.

Every week a little man with a pointy nose and a thin mustache that stuck out on both sides of his face came to the house. He was an accountant and helped Papa to keep his bills and income straight. Hansje liked to stand close by him and watch him as he wrote down numbers in columns. When the accountant wrote words, he just put his fountain pen on the paper and wrote the words. But when it came to writing a number, he always held his pen just above the paper and pretended to write the number in the air, then he put the pen on the paper and wrote the number. Every time. For every number. Hansje thought it was very funny, but he didn't laugh. He knew money and accounting were very serious. Just like church.

Once a month, the accountant also figured out how much tax Papa had to pay and how much was left to buy food, clothes, and things. Pretty soon it was clear that to buy the one-way boat tickets; Papa would have to sell the car and the house. But that was okay, Hansje knew Papa was ready to do that because one day he overheard Papa talking to a customer who was standing there eating a salted herring.

"Why do you want to emigrate?" the customer asked.

"I just want to get out of this country because there is no future here for my five children. I want to give them a chance to get a good education, and start a business or work at a good job and have their own houses. With all the taxes here they'll never get ahead, no matter how hard they work."

It made Hansje feel pretty good to know that Papa and Mama were ready to sell everything and leave their parents, their brothers and sisters, and all their friends. And then travel to a foreign land where they only knew Uncle Gabe and his family. And start all over again with nothing, even having to learn a new language, just so that he and Jannie and his little brother, Wobbie, and baby sisters, Bea and Annie, would be able to have a better life.

One day Hansje's whole family had to go to the hospital to have chest x-rays done. Papa explained to Hansje that Canada wanted people to come and was asking for healthy, hardworking people. Canada didn't want anyone who had bad diseases like tuberculosis. Hansje knew that was a bad disease because an uncle had died from it right after the war. And that's why everyone had to bring an x-ray photo of their chest to prove their lungs didn't have tuberculosis. Hansje stood in front of the screen with his shirt off and arms wide so that they could take his picture. When Papa held up Hansje's baby sister Annie in front of the screen, he held her under the armpits, and Mama held her feet so she wouldn't kick and move. When Hansje looked at her x-ray photo later, she looked like some skinny little animal, except that he could clearly see the safety pins holding her diaper.

When the doctor looked at Hansje's X-ray, he frowned and talked to Papa and Mama. Then they asked Hansje all kinds of questions.

"Have you been feeling feverish?"

"Have you been coughing for a long time?"

"Do you sweat a lot at night?"

But Hansje said, "No, I'm feeling fine. I had a cold last week, but I'm okay now."

The doctor kept asking questions,

"Do you sometimes shiver for no reason?

Are you feeling tired all the time?

Have you been getting skinnier?"

Hansje kept answering, "No" to all the questions. Then the doctor said,

"Take a deep breath and cough." So Hansje did. Then he asked,

"Did it hurt in your chest when you did that?" Hansje said, "No," again.

The doctor and Papa talked to each other for a while as they were looking at Hansje's x-ray. Then Papa came to him and said, "The doctor is going to take another x-ray of you. There is a small blurry spot on one lung which means nothing, but if some official sees it, they might make trouble and make you have another x-ray and we might miss the boat.

So Hansje took his shirt off again, and the doctor

made him hold his hands over his head this time, and also turn slightly to one side. Then he took the X-ray, and when they checked the photo, he couldn't see the blurry spot anymore. It was probably behind a rib. So, Papa was happy, and everyone went home.

But their troubles were not yet over.

37 Hansje Leaves Holland to go to Canada

When the time got close to leave Holland and go to Canada, Papa got some carpenters to come and measure the furniture and make some big shipping crates. He wanted to take the extra-long bed, the linen closet with the big mirror, the good chairs and table, some living room furniture, and especially the baby crib, the playpen, and the baby changing table that he had made himself. And, of course, the wall clock they had bought as a wedding present for themselves.

It was exciting to be getting ready, but it wasn't going to be easy to leave. Hansje found that out one day when Papa came in to eat some lunch. He had just started eating when the phone rang in the hallway. Papa went out, chewing and swallowing quickly so he could answer it. A few minutes later, he was back, his face looking pale and white and his lips pressed tightly together. His eyes were flashing with anger.

"The government tax people just found some more taxes we need to pay," he said to Mama, "but they won't let me sell the house until we have paid most of them." Suddenly he ran from the room, down the hall, and Hansje could hear him vomiting in the bathroom.

The next day Papa went to the bank to borrow some money to pay the taxes. Hansje guessed the bank didn't want to give him very much money because the next thing he knew the carpenters were gone, leaving only a small, flat crate, just enough for the bed, crib, playpen, linen closet and the clock.

The week before they left, Papa sold all the rest of their furniture and paid some of the taxes. Then he finally sold the house and paid the rest of the taxes. But now they didn't have enough money to pay for the boat tickets. Hansje knew that because he heard Papa ask his younger brother Teus if he would loan him some money. Finally, they had enough to buy the tickets.

On Monday Papa packed the last five pieces of furniture into the flat crate, nailed it shut, and sent it off to the ship on a truck. That night the whole family packed up their suitcases, left their empty house, and spent the night at Opa and Oma's house, Papa's parents.

Then, at last, on Tuesday morning, July 11, 1950, they all got up early, had breakfast after which they prayed together with Oma and Opa and the rest of the uncles and aunts that came to say goodbye. Then they loaded their stuff and themselves into a rented car and drove away. They left Hilversum, where Hansje, his brother, and sisters were born and had lived all their lives, and drove sixty-five kilometres to Rotterdam. There they would board an emigrant ship called the "Volendam."

There was a lot of confusion once they got to the dock at Rotterdam. Papa had to stand in a long line with tickets, papers, x-ray photos, and passports, while Mama sat on a big suitcase, holding baby Annie, surrounded by other suitcases that Hansje and his brother and sisters were sitting on. They were not the only people sitting on suitcases. The whole dock, the full length of the ship, was covered with women and kids sitting on suitcases waiting for the men to finish standing in line and for the signal to climb the long gangplank to the deck.

After a long time, baby Annie started to cry because she was hungry. So Mama put a shawl around her shoulders and front and breastfed her for a while until she was quiet again and went to sleep.

A mother sitting on a suitcase near them asked Mama, "How old is your baby?"

"Annie is five months old," Mama said. "Bea is two, Wobbie is six, Jannie is eight, and Hansje is twelve years old."

And Mama and Papa are really old, Hansje thought, *thirty-six and forty.*

After many hours, they let down the gangway, and everyone trooped onto the ship carrying their suitcases. Mama and the little kids were in a big cabin in the middle of the ship with some other mothers and little kids. Papa and Hansje and all the other men and boys were in a large dormitory in the front end of the ship. It took a long time to get everyone settled, but then the ship began to move, and Hansje and Papa went up on the deck to look. It was fun watching all the people waving from the dock, and he loved seeing the ships on either side of the harbor with cranes loading the ships and people working on the dock.

When they left the river channel and entered the open sea, Papa and Hansje walked to the very back of the boat, the stern, and leaned on the railing watching the land slowly get farther and farther away.

Hansje looked at Papa. He was holding onto the railing with both hands, staring beyond the white foamy wake behind the ship to the low, black shoreline as it faded into the twilight of evening.

Suddenly the bell rang calling everyone to go to the dining room for supper. But Papa didn't move. Hansje looked up at Papa's face; his eyes were glaring at the land where he was born and where he had lived for forty years.

The land where he grew up in Opa and Oma's house with six brothers and two sisters. The land where he had married Mama and had six kids, one of which died while still a baby. The land where he had hidden in swamps and under the floor of his house during the war to save his life. The land where he had quit school at twelve years old and gone to work and had worked ever since, for twenty-eight years.

And now he was leaving it all. He owned nothing but the clothes on his back and a few bits of furniture. His own country had taken everything from him except his family.

As the last black strip of land disappeared over the horizon, Papa cleared his throat and spat a great gob of disgust at his country. Then he took a deep breath of clean, fresh, salty air and said to Hansje,

"And now we are going to Canada!"

He took Hansje by the hand and walked briskly to the dining room. Hansje was excited to be on the way, finally. He couldn't wait to get to Canada.